Welcome to *IB Skills: A Practical Guide to ATL*. This book takes IB approaches to learning (ATL) and gives you concrete examples of how to develop and use these skills to improve your own learning. This is the guide for you if you have ever had trouble:

- remembering facts
- understanding why something is important
- getting the big picture, or
- communicating your understanding.

ATL skills can be learned, so let's move on and see how.

INTRODUCING SEVEN ATL SKILL AREAS

Approaches to learning (ATL) skills are the skills that help anyone to learn. Before you are able to learn, you need to develop an awareness of yourself as a learner. For example:

- Are you able to work well with others, but find it difficult to get started when working alone?
- Do you enjoy research, and are you good at communicating what you have found in a way that makes it clear to others?

This book will help you to improve your skills in these and other ATL areas.

Let's take a look at seven skills of ATL.

1. Organization

Time management—including using time effectively inside and outside the classroom and keeping to deadlines.

Self-management—including setting goals for yourself and coming to classes with all your materials, papers and pens, ready to learn.

Ask yourself:

- What attitude do I have towards organization?
- What organizational tools do I have? (A wall planner? A phone calendar?)
- What aspects of my organization do I need to develop? (Time management? Goal-setting? Study-planning?)
- How can I best organize myself? (By writing every assignment deadline into my calendar? By getting out library books three weeks early?)

2. Collaboration

Working in groups—including knowing how to ask others to support you, to take responsibility yourself within the group, to adapt to different roles and to help resolve conflicts.

Demonstrating teamwork and accepting others—including analysing others' ideas, listening to others' ideas, respecting different points of view and using ideas critically.

Personal challenges—including respecting cultural differences, negotiating goals and limitations with peers and with teachers.

Ask yourself:

- How well do I work with others?
- What successes have I had when I have worked with others?
- How can I improve how I work with others, and make it easier for them to work with me?

3. Communication

Literacy—including being informed and informing others, and reading and understanding a variety of different texts.

Being informed—getting the details from many different types of media.

Informing others—including presentation skills using a variety of media.

Ask yourself:

- What communication tools do I use?
- Which ways of communicating do I need to improve on?

4. Information literacy

Finding information—from a variety of sources using many different methods, and identifying valid and reliable primary and secondary sources.

Choosing and organizing information—deciding what you want to use, identifying points of view, bias and weaknesses, and making connections between a variety of sources.

Referencing—including the use of citing, footnotes and referencing of sources.

Ask yourself:

- How can I find information?
- How do I know if the information I find is reliable?
- What will I do with this information?

5. Reflection

Self-awareness—including seeking out positive criticism, thinking about what you find difficult.

Self-evaluation—including writing journals and reflecting at different stages in the learning process.

Ask yourself:

- How do I reflect? (By looking back over my notes? By figuring out where I went wrong in the past?)
- How have my reflections helped me learn? (Have I stopped repeating the same mistakes?)
- What other reflection tools and resources can help me?

6. Thinking

Generating ideas—including the use of brainstorming.

Planning—including storyboarding and outlining a plan.

Inquiring—including questioning and challenging information and arguments, developing questions, using the inquiry cycle.

Applying knowledge and ideas—including using logical arguments.

Identifying problems—including reasoning and evaluating solutions to problems.

Creating new ideas—through considering a problem from many different points of view.

Ask yourself:

- How do I think? (In words? Pictures? Feelings?)
- What tools can help me think in different ways? (Thinking strategies for critical or creative essays?)
- What planning tools do I have? (Analysing assignments into component parts? Timetabling?)

7. Transfer

Making connections—including using knowledge, understanding and skills across subjects to create products or solutions, applying skills and knowledge in unfamiliar situations.

Inquiring—using different points of view to develop various perspectives.

Ask yourself:

- What are the "big ideas" of each of the different subjects?
- Do the "big ideas" of the subjects overlap?
- How can I use my knowledge, understanding and skills across subjects?

WHAT IS LEARNING?

Is it:

- thinking
- understanding
- remembering
- improving
- gaining knowledge
- applying knowledge
- transferring knowledge?

Or is it all of the above?

Learning is change—moving from one state of being to another, hopefully in a positive direction. That's learning. We learn from our own experiences and we learn from other people's experiences.

Think of someone you know who you think of as a good learner. Someone who is doing well at school in a lot of subjects. What are some of the things they do that help them to be a successful learner?

Do they:

- concentrate well in class
- take good notes
- keep themselves motivated and get work done on time
- focus in class (while the teacher is talking)
- actively participate in class discussions and activities
- engage in the learning during class?

And are they good at:

- planning out assignments
- writing all sorts of different essays and research reports
- finding the right resources
- asking the right questions
- studying for exams?

Learning is not magic. It happens through the application of effective skills, called **learning skills**. Students who have good learning skills are able to:

- process information better
- find better resources
- put together better work for assessment, and
- earn better grades.

They have a huge advantage over students who don't use those same skills.

Anyone can learn how to learn more effectively and efficiently. This book has been created to teach you how.

THREE TYPES OF LEARNING SKILLS

Learning skills can be divided up into cognitive, affective and metacognitive skills.

Cognitive skills are those that are most useful in helping you acquire new knowledge or skills.

Affective skills are those that help you gain greater control over aspects of learning, such as motivation and self-concept.

Metacognitive skills are the "umbrella" skills that drive the whole learning improvement process and through which the greatest improvements in academic performance can be achieved.

Let's look at these three skills in more detail.

Cognitive skills

Cognitive skills help you with processing information and retrieval. They also help with study habits and study skills. The following cognitive skills have been shown worldwide to bring about the greatest improvements in learning and academic achievement in general.

Metacognitive skills:
Metacognition simply means the higher function of thinking. This is where you are trying out new learning strategies, monitoring their effectiveness, making changes where necessary and continually improving your learning process.

Multi-sensory techniques are memory techniques where a memory is stored using more than one sense—for example, in pictures plus sounds plus action.

- Memory techniques—mnemonics, **multi-sensory techniques**, visualization, review
- Organizing, transforming and summarizing information—mindmapping, spider diagrams, graphic organizers
- Structural writing planners for different types of essays, scientific reports, academic papers, research reports—organizing, writing, editing and revising
- Time management—general task management and specific use for timelining assignments, exam preparation
- Self-assessment—judging the quality of your own work and giving yourself a grade
- Note-making—both for notes in class and for summarizing notes for study
- Goal-setting—deciding on learning goals, breaking goals down into manageable tasks, following through until goals are achieved
- Questioning—identifying gaps in your own understanding and asking the right questions to help fill in those gaps
- Working out how you learn best—using your own experience to work out where, when and how you learn best, what types of teaching styles and learning styles work best for you

You will learn all of these key skills by working through this book.

Affective skills

These skills enable you to gain some control over your mood, your motivation and what we tend to call "attitude". These are the skills necessary to build resilience in learning, to learn to deal effectively with any setbacks and difficulties on the road to success, to learn how to bounce back, make changes and persevere. The following affective skills have been found to be the most successful at improving learning and academic achievement.

- Developing persistence and perseverance
- Learning to focus and concentrate
- Overcoming distractions
- Reducing anxiety—especially in tests and exams
- Practising delayed gratification—learning to put off rewards until the work is done
- Managing self-talk—the way you talk to yourself inside your head

Metacognitive skills

The MYP reflective cycle already incorporates the metacognitive function.

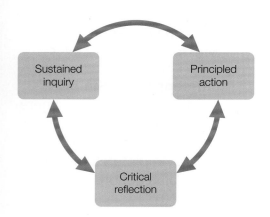

All you have to do is use this cycle to monitor the effectiveness of all the new things you are going to try out. This will help you to learn more easily and more effectively once you have finished this book.

Some of these skills will also be addressed in this book, and your teachers may well take you through some exercises to help you develop these skills.

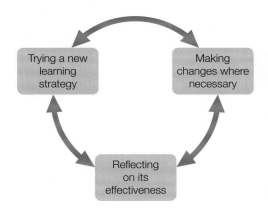

LEARNING STYLES

Before you get to different skills chapters, you need to understand a few things about yourself as a learner and about the functioning of your brain and mind.

Learning style 1: Sensory style

Have you ever noticed how you represent information in your mind?

Tomorrow, instead of going to classes you are going skiing! Your teacher has arranged for a helicopter to land in your school grounds tomorrow morning and you and all your classmates are going to get in and it is going to lift off and fly all of you to the nearest snowy mountain. It will be full of cold-weather gear and skis and you are going to put all that stuff on and the helicopter will land on the top of a mountain and you will get to ski or snowboard all the way down the mountain to the bottom. You will then get to play in the snow, go sledging and do as much skiing as you want all day. In the evening you will go to a great restaurant with a big log fire where you will get to eat a delicious meal of all the best foods you could possibly imagine and then you will get back in the helicopter and it will fly you home again and drop you off at your house.

What happened when you read this passage?

Did you see pictures in your mind—maybe a helicopter, a mountain, snow and ice?

Did you hear any sounds—maybe the sound of a helicopter, or the sound of skis rushing down a mountain, or maybe you noticed you said something to yourself?

TIPS

No person learns in only one way. Everyone can use all three ways to learn, but you may find you have a preferred method. Some people have a very strong preference for one sensory mode of thinking, some have a medium preference and some have virtually no preference at all (they can easily use any way to learn).

Did you notice any feelings arising while you were reading—whether emotions such as a feeling of enjoyment or excitement or maybe even fear, or physical feelings such as cold from the snow, or maybe feelings of action or movement, or maybe you even imagined tastes and smells?

You are probably able to imagine all those things but once you start to explore your own thinking you may discover that there is one way that you prefer to represent information in your mind.

If you do discover your preferred technique or way of representing information, you can use this knowledge to start to plan methods for learning and studying that will work best for you. If you study according to the learning preferences of your mind then information is likely to be absorbed, understood and remembered more effectively.

These ways of representing information in your mind can be grouped into three main sensory styles:

- **visual**—a preference to use your eyes to learn
- **auditory**—a preference to use your ears to learn
- **kinesthetic**—a preference to use your hands, whole body or emotions to learn.

	Thinking in:	Prefer to learn by:	Sensory style:
	pictures	looking	visual
	sounds	listening and talking	auditory
	feelings	doing	kinesthetic

The best way to discover how you prefer to learn is to notice moments when you learn something new, then ask yourself:

- What happened in that moment that is different from other moments when I did not learn something so well?
- Did I ask for a better explanation?
- Was there a visual diagram?

If you can work that out, then you can start to discover what your sensory style of learning is.

ACTIVITY

ATL skills: reflection, thinking

Time: 10 minutes

Group or Individual

LEARNING FROM EXPERIENCE 1

Fill in the blanks in the next two tables.

One new thing that I learned recently was …	Where was I?	About what time of day was it?	How was I being taught—pictures, diagrams, listening, discussing, hands-on, other activity?	Who/what helped me to understand?

One time I noticed recently that I wasn't learning well was ...	Where was I?	About what time of day was it?	How was I being taught—pictures, diagrams, listening, discussing, hands-on, other activity?	I found it difficult to learn because ...?

Reflection on your learning style

Think about what is going on around you when you are learning well and when you are not. Think about those three sensory styles of learning—learning by seeing, hearing and doing. Look for the differences between these two tables.

What are the key differences between moments when you learn well and moments when you don't?

Does it appear that any one way of learning seems to work best for you or is the most/more difficult for you?

ACTIVITY

LEARNING FROM EXPERIENCE 2

Copy both tables into the back of your homework diary or another notebook and try to add in one example on each table every day for as long as you can. At the end of the time period, summarize the information, look for trends, and try to find out how you appear to learn most effectively.

In these tables you are not just catching sensory data, you are also considering things such as time of day, place and people. These are also parts of your total learning style, which we call your "environmental preferences".

ATL skills: reflection, thinking

Time: 5 minutes every day, summing up and reporting back 1 hour for a whole class

Group or Individual

Learning style 2: Environmental preferences

The second part of your learning style you could think about is where, when and with whom you study best, including temperature, time of day, noise, distractions. These define your environmental preferences, which are important.

If you put your **sensory** and your **environmental** preferences together you are starting to build up your real learning style.

Your learning style is not necessarily the way you learn best. It is simply the way you prefer to learn—at the moment! And that may change.

TIPS

The trick with learning style is to try out different learning strategies, different ways to learn different subjects, and to pick strategies that do **both** of the following:

- suit you best, and
- achieve the best results.

The more you understand about your present learning style, the more you can make changes to ensure that your style of learning is the most effective and efficient it can possibly be. (More about this in Chapter 7, "Assessments, tests and exams".)

ACTIVITY

ATL skills: reflection, thinking

 Time: 5–15 minutes

  Individual or whole class

ENVIRONMENTAL VARIABLES QUESTIONNAIRE

Read each question and choose one answer only—the answer that suits you best. There is no right or wrong answer and you might even choose two answers for one question, depending on the situation. The aim of this exercise is simply to get you thinking about where you learn best—your learning environment.

When I am studying or doing homework at home, to get my best work done:

1. Sound—I prefer ...
   a. no noise at all, total silence
   b. some background noise (for example, music)
   c. constant background noise.
2. Light—I prefer ...
   a. bright light to work
   b. general room lighting
   c. dim light.
3. Temperature—I like the room to be ...
   a. very warm
   b. just warm
   c. cool.
4. Setting—I like my workplace to be ...
   a. a firm chair/at a desk
   b. a soft chair/at the table
   c. on the bed or on the floor.
5. People—I prefer to work ...
   a. alone
   b. with a friend
   c. with an adult who can help me
   d. in a group.
6. Time of day—I prefer getting my school work done ...
   a. as soon as I arrive home from school
   b. after dinner
   c. late in the evening
   d. early the next day, before school starts.

Learning style 3: Multi-sensory learning

Whatever your preferred way of learning— seeing, hearing or doing—if you use all three ways, then your preference really doesn't matter. If you learn in a **multi-sensory** manner you will automatically process your learning in the way that suits you best and also in the other two sensory ways as well. This will mean that your learning is represented in your mind in every possible way, so you will understand it and remember it better.

Imagine if you could learn in all three ways, with things to see, hear and do in every subject. Learning would be easier. In Chapter 7 "Assessments, tests and exams", you will find a study and learning technique that is visual **and** auditory **and** kinesthetic. If you use this study technique your learning style will be catered for— whatever it is. You will get the information in the way that suits you best, as well as all the other ways—real multi-sensory learning.

Another benefit of learning all your subjects in all three ways is that, by practising learning in the ways that suit you as well as the ways that don't, you get better at learning in every possible way.

This is the real aim of learning to learn—helping you to become a more flexible learner. The most brilliant learner is someone who can learn from anyone or anything, in any place, at any time, through any medium, using any technology, in any sensory mode: someone with great learning skills who can take full advantage of any learning situation.

IMPROVING MEMORY

TEST YOUR MEMORY

Try reading over the following list three times:

basketball	chocolate	boat
dustbin (trashcan)	chicken	scissors
fence	broom	grass
rabbit	lake	hammock.

Now close this book and try writing down as many of those items as you can remember on a separate piece of paper.

How many did you manage to remember?

If you didn't get them all, don't worry. That's normal. Most people only activate short-term memory for an exercise like this and unfortunately short term memory doesn't work very well.

ACTIVITY

ATL skills: thinking

Time: 5–20 minutes depending on discussion

Individual or whole class

TIPS

Most people's short-term memory can only hold a maximum of nine things and is only useful for remembering things for less than a minute.

Short-term and long-term memory

Short-term memory is what you are using when you are saying something over and over to yourself inside your head or out loud in order to remember it. This is called **auditory repetition** and is unfortunately the worst possible strategy to use to remember anything—because it is a short-term memory strategy.

If you want to remember more than nine things for more than one minute you need to use your long-term memory rather than your short-term memory. Long-term memory is what you use when you remember things by their context—in other words, what they are connected to, or associated with, in your mind.

Remember back to what you were doing during your country's last big national holiday—for example, last New Year's Eve. Notice how that memory comes back.

Can you bring back to mind:

- pictures—what the scene looked like, who was there, where you were?
- sounds—people's voices, music, children, other sounds?
- skin sensations—whether it was hot or cold, windy or calm?
- feelings—whether you were happy, content, excited, worried, sad?
- tastes and smells—what you ate?

For most of you that will be an easy memory to recall because when you experienced it you were using so many different senses. As a result, it is placed in a multi-sensory context. Our contextual memory is our most natural and easiest memory to use, whereas remembering things in isolation stored with only one sense requires much more effort and is much less reliable.

In the previous exercise you would have remembered more of the words if you had been able to feed them directly into your long-term memory. For a list of words like these you can connect each one separately to experiences or memories from your own life, or you can connect them to each other in a string or a chain.

There are many different ways to do this, but for this situation one good way is to create a narrative or story to link the items together. To make this work you need to make sure that the story is vivid, as silly as possible and experienced in your imagination with all your senses.

Using your imagination

Here is the list of words again:

basketball	chocolate	boat
dustbin (trashcan)	chicken	scissors
fence	broom	grass
rabbit	lake	hammock.

Read the passage below out loud, and try to picture every scene.

You are playing basketball in a back alley using a dustbin (trashcan) as the basket when you slip and crash through an old fence and fall down a dark rabbit hole and land in a chocolate cake; a chicken comes along and pulls you out and hands you a broom and you sweep all the mess into the lake then get into a boat and use a huge pair of scissors to paddle your way across to an island covered in grass where you get into a hammock and fall asleep in the sunshine.

Imagine this story vividly. Say the story out loud to yourself again, then try writing out those 12 items again, from memory.

STORY METHOD PRACTICE

Use a dictionary or your own imagination and generate 20 nouns at random. Put them in any order and use the story technique as above to memorize the whole list.

If you are doing this as a class, make the first list with the help of a partner and make up a story. Then put your list together with your neighbour's list and see if you can connect your two stories together and remember 40 random words in order. How far can you go with this? 60 words? 80 words?

The trick is making sure that your story is represented in all three senses—there must be things to see, things to hear, and actions and movement. You will find you can remember much better than before, because you are forming vivid multi-sensory links to the information by using your imagination.

ACTIVITY

ATL skills: thinking

Time: 30 minutes

Individual or whole class

Minimum effort required

One interesting thing to notice about using your imagination as a tool for memory is that it is a system that requires minimum effort. Remembering by repetition requires a lot of stress, strain, practice and testing to get it right. Remembering by using your multi-sensory imagination involves no strain and no pain. Your imagination works best when your mind is relaxed and free to create connections between ideas.

Memory techniques

Of course, you can't use that story technique to remember all the elements in the periodic table or all the battles that Napoleon fought or all the rivers in Africa. But if you have things in your school work that you do need to memorize there are many different memory techniques available that will work for you.

These are some ways of shifting information into long-term memory in each sensory system.

Sense	Technique	Example
Visual	Recognizing patterns	Factorizing algebraic equations
	Coding memories with colour	Remembering the meaning of traffic lights
	Using exaggeration	Exaggerating a feature of somebody's face or body to help recognize them
	Cartooning	Remembering a speech as a sequence of static images like a cartoon strip
	Using familiar places as hooks for memory—method of "loci"	Placing items to be remembered visually in places around your home or on your body
Auditory	Using rhymes	If asked how many days there are in August most people will refer back to "Thirty days have September, April, June …"
	Using auditory acronyms	What are the colours of the rainbow? "Richard Of York Gave Battle In Vain"
	Rhythm and melody	Remembering words of a song or an advertising jingle
	Musical compositions	Often connected with specific memories (for example, theme music for movies, political rallies)
	Auditory pegs	Using 1 = drum, 2 = shoe, 3 = tree, etc to help remember historical dates
Kinesthetic	Physical repetition	Remembering the balance necessary to ride a bike or ski, or the sequence of complex movements for dancing, or the karta in karate
	Physical pain and emotional impact	Making kinesthetic links to many memories
	Full sensory visualization of processes and events	A powerful way to remember history and languages—involving all your body, but only in your imagination

web links

There are many websites with useful memory techniques for different subjects.

http://www.academictips.org/memory/index.html has memory techniques for learning foreign languages, for exams, for people's names, lists, words, speeches and quotations, telephone numbers, dates and much more.

http://www.taolearn.com/students.php has links to other memory technique sites.

And, of course, don't forget YouTube—search "memory techniques".

Now you have experienced some different memory techniques the last two factors you need to consider are:

ATL skills: information literacy

1. How many pieces of information can you code into memory at a time?
2. When, and how often, do you need to review in order to shift information into permanent long-term memory?

Coding

CODING INTO MEMORY

Take a few seconds to read the first set of numbers here a few times, then turn over the page and write it out somewhere.

86437

Now try and do the same with this second set of numbers.

68910496

Did you notice that there was a subtle difference in the way you tried to memorize the two groups of numbers? Did you process the first set of numbers in one piece but have to break the second number down into two or three pieces in order to memorize it? If you say the second number out loud you will notice that where you put the pauses in is where you are breaking the number into chunks. Your chunks will probably be 689-10-496, 68-91-04-96, or 6891-0496, or something else.

ACTIVITY

ATL skills: thinking

Time: 5 minutes

Individual or whole class

For most people, 5 bits of information appears to be the maximum number of bits we can code into memory in one chunk. When we go over 5 bits we tend to break the total information down into smaller chunks to absorb it—in other words, no chunk with more than 5 bits.

The important thing to realize here is that we do this chunking thing automatically when we are faced with groups of numbers, but if you were given a list of 10 historical facts or chemical names to remember you wouldn't automatically break those lists down into chunks of 5 or less. You have to learn to do this deliberately.

TIPS

For good remembering, process no more than 5 bits of information at a time. You can use your memory techniques to memorize as many things as you want in one sitting—hundreds if you need to—but make it easier for yourself by doing 5 at a time.

Reviewing

The last point in this section on memory is about reviewing information—when and how often should you go over information if you want it to stick long term?

What you are trying to overcome is your tendency to forget.

If you were given some new information in class, something you had never come across before, this graph shows how quickly you would probably forget it.

Within 8 hours of first seeing new information you are down to about 30% of the detail left, and within 2 days you are down to about 10% left.

If you haven't gone over the material you learned in class yesterday, then you can expect to only remember about 25% of it now.

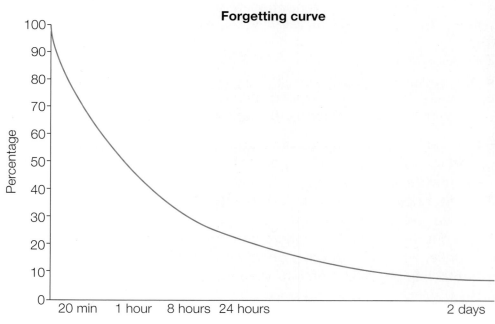

Forgetting curve

(Reprinted by permission of the Chiron Trust for Educational Research)

And if you only went through new material you learned 2 days ago once, you will only be able to remember about 10% now!

This means that when you are preparing for your next assignment or assessment, you are going to have to relearn all the information you have forgotten.

Our ability to forget rapidly, as illustrated on this graph, probably explains why many students leave all their study for tests to the last minute. They think, "Why study a month before a big test? If I am going to forget 90% of it in 2 days, maybe I should wait until the night before the test and then cram in as much as I can so that I hopefully remember some of it when I am doing the test." Sound familiar?

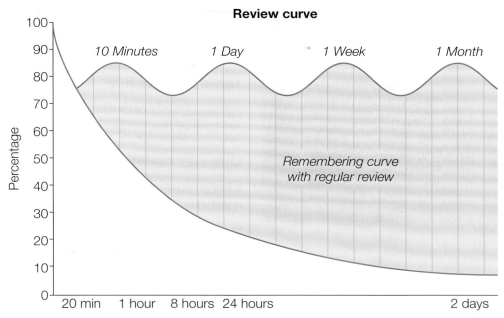

Review curve

10 Minutes   *1 Day*   *1 Week*   *1 Month*

Remembering curve with regular review

Percentage: 100, 90, 80, 70, 60, 50, 40, 30, 20, 10, 0

20 min   1 hour   8 hours   24 hours   2 days

(Reprinted by permission of the Chiron Trust for Educational Research)

Information that is only processed once through the brain soon decays and disappears. But have you ever been so fascinated by something you learned in class that you thought over the fact and told it to a friend or parent later in the day? That's the information you remember. So don't worry, you can reverse this forgetting trend and remember everything you need to for as long as you need to. You just have to understand how often and when you need to go over information in order to get it into your permanent long-term memory.

This second graph illustrates when to review what you have learned in order to shift information into permanent long-term memory.

The critical times for review (of the main points) are after:

> ten minutes
> one day
> one week, and
> one month.

TIPS

Review does not mean relearning things over and over again. It just means going over the main points to remind yourself of what you know.

This means that if you want to remember what you cover in class you need to build in these review schedules to make sure you store the information well.

Ten-minute review

As you finish one class and are packing up your gear prior to moving off to the next class just think for a moment, "What did I just learn?"

One-day review

Every night one of the most important things you can do to help your memory is to read over all the notes you took that day.

One-week review

At the end of each school week a great idea is to make a summary (maybe as a mindmap—see later in this chapter) of the key points covered in each subject.

One-month review

Then at the end of a month you can take your four weekly summaries and put them together on a big piece of paper as a one-month review.

If you do this, then by the end of the year you will have the whole year's work summarized on just a few pieces of paper, which will make it all much easier to understand and remember.

This review sequence is built into the overall study technique for tests and exams that you will find in Chapter 7 "Assessments, tests and exams".

COLLABORATIVE LEARNING

ATL skills: thinking, reflection, organization, communication, information literacy, transfer

We have just looked at how you can discover your learning style (ATL skills of thinking and reflection) and how to train your memory. You may be reading this book alone, but there is a fair chance that a lot of your learning will take place in groups and through interaction with others. Certainly, if you move on to university and into the world of work, you will be required to interact positively and productively with others so this is where collaborative skills become very important.

This involves cognitive and metacognitive skills, as you engage in learning and then think about your learning, but most of all it involves affective skills. The ability to collaborate with a number of other people who may not think the same way as you do about a task is one of the most important skills for the 21st century. In fact, it has always been an important skill, but it is only recently that collaboration towards a common goal (in this case the goal of learning) has been identified as a skill that can be learned in school.

> Learning is an active process of constructing meaning from resources (textbooks, films, news articles, teachers' notes, your own notes). When we have the chance to talk things over with other people, to present our understanding of what something means, and to listen and respond to theirs, then we are engaged in collaborative learning.

TIPS

Often you will be placed in groups by your teacher. You may not always be very happy with the people that you will be working with, but you can use this time to be actively involved in your own learning by talking to others. Think back to when you were so excited about something that you had heard, seen or done that you just had to tell somebody about it. If that person listened well, asked the right questions and was interested in what you were saying, then you will have come away feeling good, understanding more and happy to share again. If they were clearly bored and not engaged, or interrupted you with their own story, then you will have felt "shut down" and not inclined to discuss any more. It is important in a group discussion to listen as well as to speak, to ask questions that will further the group's understanding, and to work towards achieving the goal of learning about the topic or problem presented.

One way to find out what you have in common with other group members is to make a quick list of things you like doing, favourite foods, your learning style, sports you like to play, good movies, music you prefer, etc. Discuss these with other members of the group, as they discuss their preferences with you. Then create a group list, finding things that a couple, or all of you, have in common. You will be surprised at the commonalities in even the most apparently diverse group.

ACTIVITY

ATL skills: reflection, collaboration

 Time: 10 minutes

 Individual

ANALYSING MY ATTITUDE

Reflect for a moment on your own attitude towards collaborative learning.

1. When working in groups, which role do you find yourself taking?
    A. A leadership role—I steer things.
    B. A follower role—I like to let others talk first and say what I think later.
    C. An observer role—I prefer just to listen and take my own notes.
2. When given a difficult problem in class, which approach do you prefer?
    A. I suggest possible strategies for finding the answer.
    B. I listen and respond to the ideas of others.
    C. I work on it alone.
3. If one of the group members is not doing any work, what do you do?
    A. I point this out to them and say that all of us are relying on each other.
    B. I try to agree with the other members what to do about this.
    C. I do nothing—it's not my problem.
4. Given the free choice, when reviewing for an assessment, test or exam, how would you rather work?
    A. I like to organize a study group and learn together with friends.
    B. I like to join a group sometimes and study alone at other times.
    C. I prefer to study alone.
5. When working in a group, do you prefer it to be composed of:
    A. People who think the same as me.
    B. People who have a mix of different opinions.
    C. I don't mind.

As you might have worked out:

Mostly As—you are a definite collaborator, but be sure to let others take the lead sometimes.

Mostly Bs—you enjoy learning with others. Be ready to step forward into a leadership role occasionally.

Mostly Cs—you really prefer to learn alone. Do give collaborative learning a try—you might benefit from it.

Tools for collaborative learning

Mindmaps

Mindmaps can be created collaboratively, where each person takes responsibility for one part of the map. See http://www.thebrain.com/products/personalbrain for a free download of mindmapping tools.

How to draw a mindmap

- **Start** in the middle of a blank page, writing or drawing the idea you intend to develop. Landscape orientation for the page usually works best.
- **Develop** the related sub-topics around this central topic, connecting each of them to the centre with a line.
- **Repeat** the same process for the sub-topics, generating lower-level sub-topics as you see fit, connecting each of those to the corresponding sub-topic.

ACTIVITY

PRINCIPLES OF MINDMAPPING—MINDMAPPED!

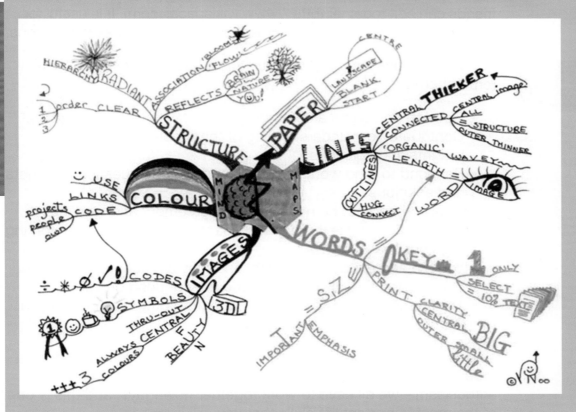

See Chapter 7 on preparing for tests and examinations for more on mindmapping.

Some more recommendations

- **Use colours, drawings and symbols.** Be as visual as you can, and your brain will thank you. Mindmapping mirrors the structure of the brain, and is not linear.
- **Keep the labels as short as possible.** Keep them to a single word—or, better yet, to only a picture. Especially in your first mindmaps, the temptation to write a complete phrase is enormous, but always look for opportunities to shorten it to a single word or figure—your mindmap will be much more effective that way.
- **Vary text size, colour and alignment.** Vary the thickness and length of the lines. Provide as many visual cues as you can to emphasize important points. Every little bit helps to engage your brain. (Adapted from material at http://litemind.com/.)

Sharing documents online

This is another way to work collaboratively. Google docs (https://docs.google.com) or Box.net (http://www.box.net) are both excellent ways to do this. Then several people can share and work on the same document at the same time. A wiki is a web page that you and your friends can edit together (http://www.wikispaces.com). It is useful for sharing revision tips and for commenting on each other's contributions.

ATL skills: collaboration

For collaborative learning to occur, a few basics have to be remembered.

- Develop and share a common goal.
- Contribute your understanding of the problem: questions, insights and solutions.
- Respond to, and work to understand, others' questions, insights and solutions.
- Conflict need not be negative—disagreement and working together to resolve it are a necessary part of progress in working together.
- You are accountable to others, and they are accountable to you.
- You are dependent on others, and they depend on you.
- Think creatively and use knowledge from other subjects in your learning.

Your teacher will have different activities that allow you to work as a group and improve your collaborative skills. Enter into them with enthusiasm—we all have to work together nowadays, and this is one of the most important life skills that you will learn.

KEY POINTS OF THE CHAPTER

ATL skills

- Organization
- Collaboration
- Communication
- Information Literacy
- Reflection
- Thinking
- Transfer

The main stages of learning about learning

- Developing the learning skills
- Identifying your learning style(s)
- Training your memory
- Strengthening your collaborative learning

Useful websites

For questionnaire-based analysis of learning styles some examples are:

http://www.engr.ncsu.edu/learningstyles/ilsweb.html. Index of learning styles questionnaire, North Carolina State University.

http://www.vark-learn.com/english/page.asp?p=younger. A guide to learning styles for younger people, plus questionnaire, VARK.

http://people.usd.edu/~bwjames/tut/learning-style/. "What´s your Learning Style?". University of South Dakota.

For memory techniques try the following websites:

http://www.academictips.org

http://www.youtube.com/watch?v=sBzYK8Qwnps

http://www.youtube.com/watch?v=DhdfBMRNMLU&feature=related

For other useful tips try the following websites:

http://www.box.net. Very useful for sharing documents for collaborative working, or for uploading to a blog or website.

https://docs.google.com. Very useful for sharing documents for collaborative working or for uploading to a blog or website.

http://litemind.simplusmedia.com. Lots of mindmapping tips.

http://www.taolearn.com Lots of links to free websites for all school subjects as well as tips for how to take notes and how to study

http://www.thebrain.com. Useful site for study skills and learning styles.

http://www.youtube.com. Just search "learning skills" or "memory".

ESSAY WRITING SKILLS

In this chapter you will learn:

- which ATL skills will support you in writing essays
- the importance of academic honesty and time management
- how to use graphic organizers
- how to plan and write three main types of essay—narrative/descriptive, persuasive/argumentative and analytical.

Nothing is scarier than a blank sheet of paper. Well, maybe the only thing scarier is a blank sheet of paper and a deadline of tomorrow (or yesterday)! The point is that essay-writing is a learned skill that includes many of the ATL skills. It can be learned through practice.

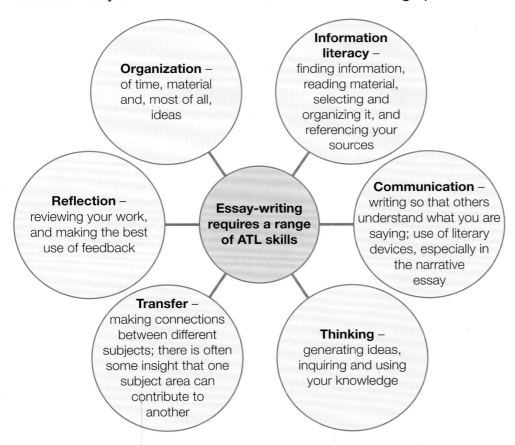

Organization – of time, material and, most of all, ideas

Information literacy – finding information, reading material, selecting and organizing it, and referencing your sources

Reflection – reviewing your work, and making the best use of feedback

Essay-writing requires a range of ATL skills

Communication – writing so that others understand what you are saying; use of literary devices, especially in the narrative essay

Transfer – making connections between different subjects; there is often some insight that one subject area can contribute to another

Thinking – generating ideas, inquiring and using your knowledge

The most important factors to bear in mind when essay-writing are time management and academic honesty, so we will look at these first.

TIME MANAGEMENT

Throughout this chapter you will see references to drafting, reading and reviewing your essay. You can't do this if you don't have the time! Essay-writing is not a simple process, so it is more useful to plan it in advance, especially when research is required. Starting early helps avoid unforeseen problems such as not being able to find immediately the literature or evidence you need, or having to ask for an extension if you are sick for a day. It is also useful to divide the writing process into several days, as interesting ideas need time to "mature". Going backwards and forwards to the writing over a period of a few days will often produce the best results.

Here are some tips on managing your time.

The essay assignment

- When you are given the essay assignment, make sure that you understand it, and can write the title out in your own words. If you can't, quickly ask your teacher for an explanation.

Research

- Allow several days for this, and use a graphic organizer or planning template of some kind. (See examples later in this chapter.) Make sure what you select is relevant to the topic.

Drafting

- See below for how to do this. The question is *when* to do it? You can start your draft while still researching by entering the relevant information straight into your planning template or graphic organizer, and putting the references at the end. Try and complete your draft very quickly after finishing your research.

web links

Useful search engines that you can use by typing in key words from your essay topic or title can be found at http://netforbeginners.about.com/od/navigatingthenet/tp/top_10_search_engines_for_beginners.htm. An easy site to navigate for factual information is http://www.factmonster.com.

Your school may also have subscriptions to sites such as ERIC (http://www.eric.ed.gov) or *Britannica Online Encyclopedia* (http://www.britannica.com/).

Ask your school librarian to help you find print or internet resources.

Deadlines

If the deadline for your draft is Thursday, try to have it done by Wednesday. If there is no draft deadline, but you are to submit your final essay by Thursday, then try and have the draft completed by the Friday before. The logic is that you have a weekend to look it over, Monday at school to get further feedback from friends and your teacher, and then Monday and Tuesday night to complete it with a day in hand. This avoids stress and allows you to do your very best.

Problem-solving strategies

Problems happen. But for every problem there is a solution (apart from panicking!). Here is a list of common problems that prevent students from handing in essays on time, complete with their solutions.

You lose your work (either hard copy or e-copy)

Tell your teacher quickly and try to find a back-up copy. Otherwise, start writing from your notes template again.

Next time: Remember to keep a back-up as you write. Google docs (https://docs.google.com), or a similar site, is useful for this.

You are sick and your essay is due tomorrow.

Get a note from a parent to take into school the next day. Do not try to finish the essay if you are really ill. It will not be your best work.

Next time: Have a day in hand, so you can send your essay in with a friend, or even email it to your teacher, or give your teacher access to it on the online docs site.

You are stuck—your mind is a blank and the page is still empty.

Ask for help from a friend or a teacher. Just talk it through, starting with the title and any thoughts and ideas you have. Look back at the research notes. Maybe you have lost focus on the topic or question.

Next time: Try to talk your essay over regularly with friends and family (or even with yourself in front of the mirror) before you get to this stage.

You thought your essay was OK, but now you have read the draft and it is so boring.

Get the opinion of someone you trust. (Not someone who will just tell you what you want to hear!) Reread it and be sure that you are not just in a bad mood. Rewrite where necessary, adding vivid detail and/or logical argument that will engage your reader.

Next time: Check your draft as you go along and try to place yourself in the mind of your reader.

1. Think of a problem, a solution and a way to prevent it from happening again. This way you are in control of your own learning.

2. Avoid the "paralysis by analysis" of writer's block. Don't worry about spelling, grammar or paragraphs if you feel blocked—just do it! Write first and proofread later.

ACADEMIC HONESTY

ATL skills: literacy

Academic honesty just means that you say where you got your ideas and quotes from. Every time you quote from somebody else's work, or use one of their ideas, you need to reference this using one of the conventional formats for referencing and citation. (See http://www. easybib.com.)

Failure to do this is called "plagiarism", and the penalties for this are severe, including failing to gain any formal credit, as no school allows plagiarism. Many cases of plagiarism happen through simple mistake. You take notes as you research and forget later that what you are writing has come from somebody else. By the time you have written your draft and then your final essay, the words feel like your own. To avoid this always note down the reference of what you are writing straight away. Even if the words are not quoted, if the ideas are somebody else's you must still reference them. The same rules apply for pictures, maps, diagrams. If they have been taken from other sources, then this needs to be documented.

Sometimes, if your written English is not very good, it can be tempting to copy and paste someone else's words in place of your own. After all, they are just saying so well what you are trying to say. **Avoid** this. You will develop a writing style of your own. Copying and pasting others' work just because you can't think how to say what you want to say is still plagiarism. If you reference the words, it is not, but the essay has to be yours: it cannot be full of the ideas and words of others.

Your school will probably have asked you to sign an academic honesty statement when you enrolled and will almost certainly have a school guide to research and academic honesty. Again, ask your librarian—and if there is not one, then the IB publishes a guide to academic honesty.

Don't plagiarize—you can do better than that!

ACTIVITY

IN YOUR OWN WORDS

Rewrite the following passage in your own words. (Remember, you will still have to reference the ideas, but you will not be directly quoting.)

A vital ingredient in good essay-writing is time management. Without effective time management a student cannot produce an excellent essay. Time is important for planning (ATL skill: organization); researching ideas (ATL skills: information literacy and thinking); drafting the essay using a template or graphic organizer (ATL skills: organization, thinking, communication and transfer); reviewing the essay (ATL skill: reflection). So, plan in advance to avoid last-minute stress and to make sure that your essay does you justice.

ATL skills: thinking, reflection, organization, communication, information literacy

Time: 5–10 minutes

Individual

THE STAGES OF WRITING AN ESSAY

Essay-writing—as easy as baking a cake

Excellent essay writers are made, not born. Cooks learn to bake the perfect cake through practice, and you need to practise essay-writing to learn how to write the perfect essay. This means gathering the ingredients, and combining them in the correct proportions—in other words, *using* them, to bake the cake that is exactly the right flavour to meet your needs. Just like a cake, an essay has a formula, or recipe. However, also just like a cake, some creativity will improve an essay, so don't be afraid to experiment a little. Let's start baking!

1. Gathering material

In order to create your essay, you need to use the correct ingredients to answer the question. What type of essay is it? Do you have to analyse a character, write your opinion on something, describe a book that you have read, or maybe explain an historical event? Whatever it is, gather your ingredients (materials and ideas) and organize them. This is where graphic organizers can be helpful. http://freeology.com/graphicorgs/ is a site that has many free, downloadable and printable graphic organizers, such as the one on the next page.

ATL skills: organization, information literacy, thinking

Who, What, When and Where

What

Who

Topic

When

Where

Focus on the essay title. When you go to your kitchen cupboard you might find cheese, but if you are making a fruit cake you would not use it. When you research an essay you will come across many sources that might be interesting, but if they don't help you answer the question, or aren't relevant, then don't use them. You can always save them for later!

Remember at this stage to collect references for every idea or quote you find that you might want to use in your essay. References are formatted according to a particular convention. A site such as http://www.easybib.com can make this much easier. See the previous section on academic honesty for more about this.

2. Planning your essay

Getting started is the hardest part, but don't let that blank sheet of paper put you off. Start by planning an outline of your essay. Again, a graphic organizer may be helpful. Create an outline of your essay.

ATL skills: organization, thinking, information literacy, transfer

So, first, what type of essay are you going to write? If you don't know, now is the time to find out. There are many different types of essays, but they fall into three main categories:

- Narrative/descriptive—telling a story/saying what something is like
- Persuasive/argumentative—making an argument (this includes evaluative essays and compare and contrast essays)
- Analytical—an informed interpretation of, and response to, the ideas within a text

3. Writing your draft/essay

ATL skills: organization, thinking, communication, transfer, reflection

Every essay has to have a structure: a beginning, a middle and an end. These are also described as the introduction, the content and the conclusion. The length of your essay will vary with your course requirements, but it is usual for essays in the MYP to be between 500 and 1,000 words in length. Structure is looked at in more detail below for narrative/descriptive essays and persuasive/argumentative essays.

4. Reviewing your draft/essay

ATL skills: reflection

It is likely that you will have been given the chance to hand in a draft before writing your final essay. Even if you have not, what you have written will need to be reviewed and reflected upon—by you, your friends and, hopefully, by your teacher as well. This is a very important, and often forgotten, stage.

We will now look in more detail at three different types of essays: narrative/descriptive, persuasive and analytical essays. Before doing so, it is important to point out that there are differences in the way people from different cultures write essays. Here we look at an English approach to writing essays which has sometimes been characterized as being very direct. You may have been taught to approach writing essays differently. If so, **it is important to point out that there are differences in rules, styles and approaches to writing essays within different cultures**. Be sure to consult your teacher for clarification before you begin writing.

NARRATIVE/DESCRIPTIVE ESSAYS

Narrative/descriptive essays tell stories. They are often told from the author's point of view, and use sensory details and literary devices to engage the reader in the author's feelings, or the feelings attributed to the character. The narrative essay often relies on personal experiences and uses the conventions of storytelling: plot, character, setting, climax and ending. These are the essays that you write most often in your languages classes. They are "creative writing", because you are creating the story.

Your job in writing a narrative/descriptive essay is to make the strange and foreign deeply personal and familiar, so the reader can imagine it happening to him or her and can identify with your main character's feelings.

Gathering material for your narrative/descriptive essay

Narrative/descriptive essays still need you to gather material for your background. Ask yourself the following questions.

- What are you writing about?
- What have other writers had to say about this topic?
- How will your plot develop?
- What additional information do you need in order to add realistic detail to your setting (if this is fiction) or to remind yourself what the conditions were like (if this is fact)?

Looking at narrative writing by famous authors will often help you to get the feel for this genre. Authors to look out for are Roald Dahl, Ervin Lázár, Paul Jennings, Eva-Lis Wuorio, Beverley Naidoo, Mark Twain and Isabel Allende, but there are many others.

"If story is not about the hearer he [or she] will not listen … The strange and foreign is not interesting— only the deeply personal and familiar." John Steinbeck (1952)

Planning your narrative/descriptive essay

The content of your narrative essay will usually include the following.

Theme: What is your essay about? Decide on a theme, or you may have been given a title by your teacher. You will develop this further and support it with more interesting information. See http://www.brainpop.com/english/writing/mainidea/ for an excellent video on finding the main idea of an essay.

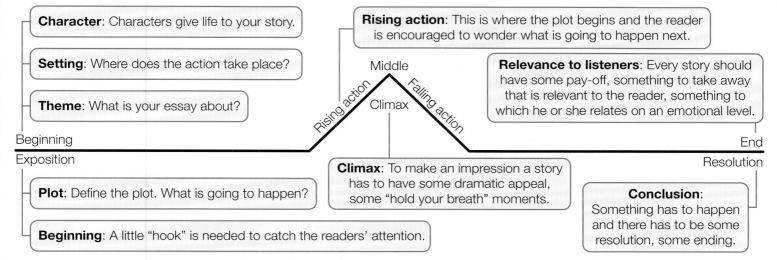

Character: Characters give life to your story.

Setting: Where does the action take place?

Theme: What is your essay about?

Beginning

Exposition

Plot: Define the plot. What is going to happen?

Beginning: A little "hook" is needed to catch the readers' attention.

Middle

Rising action

Climax

Falling action

Rising action: This is where the plot begins and the reader is encouraged to wonder what is going to happen next.

Relevance to listeners: Every story should have some pay-off, something to take away that is relevant to the reader, something to which he or she relates on an emotional level.

End

Resolution

Climax: To make an impression a story has to have some dramatic appeal, some "hold your breath" moments.

Conclusion: Something has to happen and there has to be some resolution, some ending.

Plot: Define the plot. What is going to happen?

Below are some key elements of plot that you may want to spend some time thinking about.

In every short story or film we see a character facing a problem or a conflict. The conflict could be:

- a personal conflict (for example, a character trying to come to terms with a loss)
- a conflict between two characters or groups
- a conflict between the character and nature of their environment (for example, a person struggling at sea in a storm or a shipwrecked person trapped on an island)
- a conflict between a character/group and a supernatural or alien force (for example, humans facing the threat of invaders from another planet).

In each case the character undergoes a change whether for the better or the worse. They may even end up dying! The key is to reveal how they have been changed by the event.

TIPS

Many effective short stories cover a very short space of time. This could be from 5 minutes to a few days. By focusing on short periods of time and "exploding the moment" at key points in your story you will create more tension and interest. A common fault is to try and cover too much ground and include too much action. Many of the best stories have very little action and focus on the character(s)' thoughts and emotions as they struggle with their situation.

Character: Characters give life to your story. They are like actors in a play. You can be the main character, the "I" of the story, or maybe the title you have been given suggests someone else. The key here is to create characters who are believable. To do this make sure you have considered your techniques of characterization:

What they say and how they say it	Do characters have specific speech patterns or use certain expressions or language that sets them apart or defines them?
	To what extent do they make/use statements, questions, commands and/or exclamations and how do these convey their tone or mood? For example, someone asking lots of questions may be doubtful, uncertain or concerned.
	Turn taking/interruptions—do they interrupt to agree and show solidarity or do they interrupt other characters to show/demonstrate their authority?
	Do they dominate the conversation and/or dictate the subject matter?
	What form of address do they use in dialogue and how do these convey the status and relationships between characters (for example, calling people by their first name or by their title)?
What they don't say/ pauses/gaps/silences	Ignoring a question, ignoring a person and/or playing a passive role in conversations can reveal as much about a character as what they do say.
What others say about them	Do we see other characters making comments about your protagonist when they are present or absent from the scene? Having other characters describing or discussing the character before we meet them, can shape the reader's expectations of them.
Their thoughts	Describing the thoughts of the character(s) gives us yet another insight into their mind(s). They may be thinking differently from how they are behaving outwardly. Writing in **free indirect discourse** is one way of presenting a character's thoughts through a third person narrative.
Their interactions with other characters	Seeing a character interacting with other characters (through speech, actions, behaviour) can reveal different aspects of their personality. Are characters contrasted with another character?

Their appearance	How characters dress (the sort of clothes they wear), even their hairstyle can say something about their mood, status, or situation.
Their facial expressions	By describing their facial expressions you can communicate how they are feeling—show the reader in images rather than telling them (for example, instead of, *he was angry*, you could write, *the veins in his temples grew more pronounced and his face turned redder by the second.*
Their movements/ actions/posture/ stance/gestures	The way characters stand, move and use gestures can reveal their mood and their relationship with the person they are interacting with. For example, *He stood, towering over the boy at the desk shaking his fist. The girl shuffled into the bus shelter and curled up on the hard plastic bench.*
Their relationship to their surroundings/ different settings	Seeing a character in different settings (intimate private settings, public settings, work/school settings or at home) can reveal different aspects of their personality. Do they behave differently in different settings? Do they seem comfortable/ uncomfortable in different places? Does the setting reflect their character (isolated setting may reflect a desire to be alone or the fact a character feels alienated)?
Their relationship to a symbol	Are characters seen with a particular object or prop (for example, constantly looking at their watch, always with their dog, sitting by a fire) which reveals something about their personality?

TIPS

Basing a character on someone you know is a tactic often used by professional writers. You can adapt, and perhaps, exaggerate their certain physical features or behavioral aspects. By using someone you know well, it may help you be more specific when describing aspects such as their appearance, their habits and/or their speech pattern.

Setting: Where does the action take place? If it is somewhere "strange and foreign", how are you going to insert little touches that make it familiar to your audience? The setting can play a key role in your story. As you make your plan, you may wish to consider some of the following questions.

- Is it realistic? Are there details which make it seem like a real place? A good tactic is to describe a place you know well and can effectively recreate for a reader in images and sounds.
- Will the setting influence the plot or characters creating dramatic tension and interest (for example, a storm forcing a character to take shelter somewhere)?
- How can you bring the scene to life for the reader by appealing to their senses—using specific sounds you describe or language devices like onomatopoeia?

- Will aspects of your setting work symbolically to help convey the mood or atmosphere of a character or event (like the classic cliché of rain at a funeral reflecting sorrow)? Think about aspects of the landscape or weather that could convey symbolism (for example, different climates, seasons, different/changing light or sounds) and could be used to echo or reflect a character's mood. Let the **verbs**, **adjectives** and **adverbial phrases** convey the mood as in these examples below.
  - His footsteps echoed down the lonely corridors.
  - The dark figure stood slouched against a solitary lamp post.
  - A lone goose lifted slowly over the lake, the sound of its flapping wings echoing through the gloomy valley.
  - The waves kissed the bow, lapping the paintwork in a tender embrace.
  - The soaring towers of moisture darkened the horizon, smothering the valley in a grey blanket of charged electricity.
  - A sharp crack split the heavens sending a blue scar jabbing into the forest's centre, shattering the silence.

Beginning: A little "hook" is needed to catch the readers' attention. An unusual comment about something familiar, or something to make your readers' want to read more.

Rising action: This is where the plot begins and the reader is encouraged to wonder what is going to happen next.

Climax: To make an impression a story has to have some dramatic appeal, some "hold your breath" moments.

Relevance to listeners: Every story should have some pay-off, something to take away that is relevant to the reader, something to which he or she relates on an emotional level.

Conclusion: Something has to happen and there has to be some resolution, some ending.

Literary devices: How it all works

We will look at structuring your essay later. First, let's see how you can make your writing interesting.

You will need to support your story with description and details, and this is where the literary devices of alliteration, characterization, metaphor, simile, personification, imagery and hyperbole can come in. There are many more literary devices, but we will just look at these few, as they help us to engage our readers when we describe our experiences.

Alliteration

When two or more words in a sentence begin with the same letter or sound. This is used a lot in poetry as well as prose.

Examples

Tom touched his tongue tentatively to his teeth. (ttttt)

She walked weakly into the edge of the wheat field. (www)

Wriggling worms wound up from their dark dens beneath the summer soil. (www, dd, ss)

Characterization

Used to draw a picture of a person in the reader's imagination. It helps description. Characterization generates plot and is revealed by actions, speech, thoughts, physical appearance, as well as the other characters' thoughts or words.

Examples

My brother, a tall, stick-like figure with gentle grey eyes, regarded me carefully and began to explain his decision to move the company to Alaska.

It was hard for her to keep from smiling. I could see her lips twitching at the corner and knew that very soon she would be fighting to control her laughter.

Metaphor

A figure of speech that says that one thing is another different thing. It saves words and the reader has to find the common link.

Examples

His room was his prison.

Her mother was her whole world.

Simile

Is like metaphor, except that the comparison is made more obvious. In a simile, the words "as" or "like" are used to show the similarity.

Examples

His room is like a prison.

He worked like a dog.

The sheet is as white as snow.

Personification

Is when you give an object human qualities or abilities.

Examples

The rustling leaves whispered her name.

The mud grasped his ankle with its slimy fingers.

Imagery

When you use words to create a picture in your reader's mind.

> **Examples**
>
> *The spectacular sunset bathed the coast in its orange light.*
>
> *The elephants trampled dustily down to the dry waterhole.*

Hyperbole

The use of exaggeration to make a point.

> **Examples**
>
> *My boyfriend called my mobile phone a thousand times, but I was determined not to answer.*
>
> *He had told her a million times not to do that.*

web links

 For an example of literary devices look for the following clip on YouTube:

1. Search 'imagery and literary device' and 'university project'. You should find a video by 'melapino1'.
2. Or go to http://www.youtube.com/watch?v=DwDVmBDgubw&feature=results_main&playnext=1&list=PL784FF9616E9DE1B4

Writing your narrative/descriptive essay

Before you start writing, remember that a compelling plot with detailed description is the key to writing a successful narrative/descriptive essay.

Plot

A plot is what happens—the events that make up a story. The pattern of events should have some effect on the reader, and this is where you use your literary devices to aid description and make sure that the events do. This is also where the ATL skill of transfer comes in, as you use your knowledge from different subjects and topics to write your essay.

Compare these two pieces of writing about the same event.

I was 8 when I first went near a horse. I had always wanted to ride, but the closer I drew to the snorting beast, the more nervous I became. In reality the "beast" was a small pony called Spiderman; but then I was a small boy, and size was in the eye of the beholder. And in the twisting snakes of fear in the beholder's belly.

"Up we go. Nice and gently does it," reassured my father as he lifted me on to the shiny leather saddle. I grasped the reins tightly, together with a generous tuft of stringy mane. So far was so good. All might have remained well had my father not also decided to reassure Spiderman, with a pat on his chestnut back. He interpreted that as a command to move smartly off at a bone-shaking run. I fell forward, flung my arms desperately around his neck and began to cry. My father laughed and moved to grab the reins, but Spiderman was having none of it: he manoeuvred successfully around my father and broke into a clumsy brisk walk, lowering his head, and shaking it to dislodge the unfamiliar body by now halfway down his neck. I landed with a bump, biting my tongue in the process, and lay there, sobbing bitterly through a mouth full of blood. I was 8 when I last went near a horse.

I first went horse-riding when I was 8 years old. Although I rode a small pony, I was scared, and didn't like it at all. My father patted the pony's back, and he moved off quickly, and I fell off almost at once. I gave up and wouldn't go again.

The first piece of writing brings the experience alive, with the writer's memory of his fear, contrasted with his father's lack of empathy. I am sure that many of us can identify with moments like this. (Did you spot the literary devices? For example, "*And in the* twisting snakes of fear in the beholder's belly" uses metaphor and alliteration.) The rule for bringing the narrative alive is: "Don't just tell it. *Show* it."

ACTIVITY

ATL skills: organization, thinking, information literacy

Time: 30–40 minutes

Individual

REWRITING TO MAKE IT EXCITING (OR, FROM ZZZZZ TO AHA!)

Rewrite the following plot to engage the reader. Keep to the basic order of events, but add supporting detail using literary devices. Give your story a title, and then share it with a friend for a peer review.

I got up early on the morning of my sixteenth birthday, and walked up the street to the beach. The wind was blowing off the sea, and as I stood watching the waves, I heard someone calling out, "Help me!" I ran into the sea and dragged the struggling woman on to the sand. She was the owner of a local restaurant and was so grateful that she organized a really good party that evening for my birthday.

Now you are ready to write your excellent narrative essay!

The three stages

There are three stages to building your narrative/descriptive essay.

Introduction	Identify the importance of the experience/event.
	Begin with a paragraph that will introduce what happened and why it was important. It is also possible to begin with what happened, and leave its importance till the end. In this way the reader creates his or her own interpretation of the significance of the event.
Content	Give your readers the experience.
	Using your outline that you created during the planning stage, describe each part of your narrative. Recreate the experience for your readers by using your literary devices, details and descriptions to interest them.
Conclusion	This is the ending of your narrative essay.
	End your narrative by telling the readers the effect that the events had on you, or on the main character if this was not you. If you have done a good job your readers should really care about what happened, and why it was important.

Let's look at these three stages in more detail.

Introduction

Use "the hook"	This is the statement about your story that catches the reader's attention. It can be a quotation or a statement about what happened ("I was 15 when my life changed forever") or even a question ("What would you do if your mother left you on a park bench and never came back?").
Set the scene	Provide the information the reader will need in order to understand the essay. Who are the main characters? When and where is it taking place? Is it real or is it fiction?
Theme	This tells the reader exactly what the essay is about. It encapsulates what happened.

Content

Make it alive	A good narrative essay includes details and descriptions that help the reader understand what you or the main character experienced. Think about description, and maybe consider using all five senses to add details about what you heard, saw and felt during the event. **Example:** "My stomach dropped as the dog bared his teeth in warning at me" provides more information than: "I saw a dog when I was out walking."
Supporting details	Whether fact or fiction, experience acts as evidence. The events of the story should demonstrate the lesson learned, or the significance of the event to you or your character.
Passage of time	Writing about events and experiences using time chronologically, from beginning to end, is the most common and the clearest way to tell a story. However, you may choose to begin your story "in media res"—in the middle of events—and then work back from the beginning as many modern films and novels do. If you do this you could use flashback as a way to fill in gaps in the story and in the lives of your character(s). For example, you could begin the story at the build-up to a moment of tension and then use a flashback in the character's thoughts to reveal how the character came to be in that situation. Even if you choose not to write chronologically, use transition words such as "next", "finally", "during", "after", "when", "later" to clearly indicate to the reader the order of what happened.

Transitions

In a narrative essay, a new paragraph marks a change in the action of a story, or a move from action to reflection. Paragraphs should connect to one another. For example, the end of one paragraph might be: "I turned and ran, hoping the dog wouldn't chase me" and the start of the next might be: "There are many strategies for surviving an encounter with a ferocious dog; 'turning and running' is not one of them." The repetition of words connects the paragraphs.

Notice the change in tense as the writer reflects on the past event, from the perspective of the present. The events of most narratives are told in the past tense: "I turned and ran …" Use the present tense when reflecting on the events: "There are many strategies …"

Conclusion

The conclusion of a narrative essay includes the closing action of the event, but should also include some reflection or analysis of the significance of the event to you or your character. What lesson was learned? What was the point or moral of this story?

Some other questions you may want to consider include.

- Does your ending meet your reader's expectations or do you end with an unexpected twist and surprise them?
- Does your ending tie up all loose ends or will you leave questions unanswered?
- Does your ending create new questions for the reader?

One final detail

It is important to stop a moment and think about the structure of each paragraph. Paragraphs need a topic sentence and some supporting sentences. The topic sentence usually, but not always, comes at the beginning of the paragraph. Topic sentences make a point and the rest of the paragraph gives reasons or examples to support it.

Example

I will never go climbing alone again. With the warm sun on my back, I left my house at the foothills of the Jura mountains, equipped with my sunglasses and sun cream, my bottle of water and my climbing gear. I had forgotten how quickly the weather can change, and not taking my raincoat and warm clothing was to be an almost fatal mistake. What's more, I also failed to remember the number one rule—let somebody know where you are and when you expect to return.

The topic sentence could easily be moved from the beginning of this paragraph to the end or even the middle without affecting the meaning.

web links

 Go to this site and enjoy yourself identifying the topic sentences. http://www. internet4classrooms.com/assessment_assistance/assessment_preparation_language_ arts_topic_sentence.htm

Reviewing your narrative/descriptive essay

Once you have written your essay, do not forget this most important last step.

Leave your essay for a while, if you have the time. Then reread it yourself, checking especially for grammar and spelling mistakes. Ask a friend to read it, and make use of your teacher's comments.

Be receptive to feedback. It is part of the learning process.

PERSUASIVE/ARGUMENTATIVE ESSAYS

Now let's take a look at the second type of essay.

The purpose of a persuasive/argumentative essay is to convince the reader to agree with your viewpoint or to accept your recommendation for a course of action. This is also the type of essay that you will write in subjects such as sciences and humanities to make an argument, carefully weighing and evaluating evidence to draw your conclusion.

Gathering material for your persuasive/argumentative essay

Know what your opinion is before you start researching and gathering material to enable you to build a logical and well-supported argument. This will involve finding writers who support your stance, and examples of evidence from those who don't. Do not be tempted to gather evidence for your point of view only; it is important to have a balanced argument that looks at the evidence for the "other side" (counter-argument), even if only to dismiss it.

Take your time and be sure that you know whether the evidence you have supports the argument or the counter-argument.

Planning your persuasive/argumentative essay

For instance, you might argue that the salaries of teachers are too high. Or you might recommend that fizzy sweet drinks be banned from your school cafeteria. A successful persuasive essay will use evidence to support your viewpoint, consider opposing views and present a strong conclusion.

As a general guideline, when writing a persuasive essay:

- have a firm opinion that you want your reader to accept
- begin with a hook to get the reader's attention (just as in the narrative essay)
- offer evidence to support your opinion
- end with a restatement of what you want the reader to do or believe.

One of the simplest ways to organize your evidence in order to build your argument is to use a model like the one below, or any other organizer you find that makes it easy to plan your writing. Make sure of your facts and remember that writing an essay means that you have to understand the material. Remember the cake from the beginning of this chapter, and if you don't know what something is don't put it in!

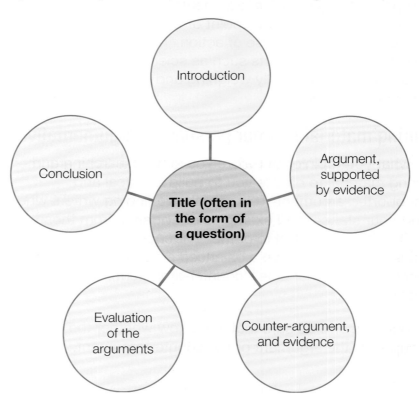

You will often need to compare one argument with another, to see where they differ and where they are the same. This next organizer can help with that.

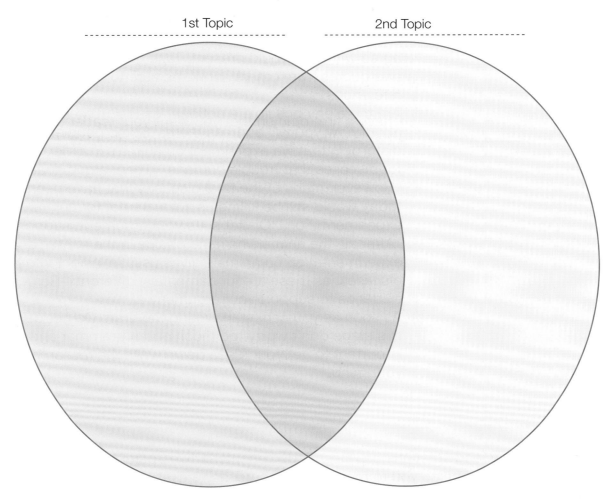

1st Topic   2nd Topic

Planning your essay means you need to build a good argument by:

- establishing evidence and taking a stance (remember to consider all the evidence you have gathered, for both the argument and counter-argument; however, unless you are going to change your position, the evidence for the counter-argument should be looked at with a plan as to how you will reject it)
- prioritizing, editing and/or sequencing the evidence in importance to build the argument
- forming and stating conclusions
- demonstrating that your conclusions are based upon the evidence
- communicating this persuasive argument in writing.

Here are some strategies to help.

a) Write out the question/title of the essay in your own words.

b) Think of the questions posed in the assignment while you are reading and researching. When you find evidence for your argument, ask yourself what evidence someone who did not agree with you would present. Take notes, and if you use ideas and quotes from others' work, be sure to keep a record of the reference.

c) Are there any possible emotional issues? If there are, think about how you will address them: "Some people find it disturbing that we experiment on animals in order to find cures for diseases that trouble humans." Then, argue against them: "However, many of the fatal diseases that have been eradicated today would still be killing us if it were not for animal experimentation." Or, if it suits your argument, support them: "After all, the animals have no choice in the matter, and experimentation on animals gives us little insight into human diseases, as these are fundamentally different." Remember to use evidence to support your argument.

d) As soon as you can, start writing the draft. Do not delay and at this stage don't worry too much about grammar and spelling. It is important to get your ideas down while the research is fresh in your mind.

web links

 See http://www.readwritethink.org/files/resources/interactives/persuasion_map/ for an interactive tool that helps you to map out your persuasive essay. Another useful site is http://www.timeforkids.com/TFK/media/hh/pdfs/ideaorganizers/persuasive_ideaorg.pdf. This site provides a graphic organizer for your ideas.

Writing your persuasive/argumentative essay

Gather your references, your materials and your plan, and then write the first draft. Sit at a large table, so that any materials that are not electronic can be arranged around you. Assume that your readers will need clear explanations. Keep the language simple, but use terms appropriate for your subject.

Now you are ready to write your draft.

Introduction	Place the argument in your first (topic) sentence. This is your opening statement, so should be strong and clear.
	Write two or three supporting sentences, including your point of view. Focus on the main points that you want to develop.
	Write a linking sentence to the **next** paragraph.
Content	a) Start with a paragraph or two outlining the argument. Make sure you have at least two pieces of supporting evidence, preferably more, organized in logical order of strength/relevance.
	b) Follow with a paragraph or two acknowledging the counter-argument—there is always evidence as well for a counter-argument. Remember in a) and b) to quote and reference sources and to remain focused. Establish a flow from paragraph to paragraph.
	c) End with a paragraph that gives an evaluation of both arguments. The final sentence of this paragraph should make it clear that the main argument is the stronger. (If you find that during your research your opinion changes, then make sure that you argue what you feel the evidence shows. Never try to argue for what you don't believe in, except as an exercise in debate.)
Conclusion	Summarize the arguments and restate your case. Compare and contrast the arguments here. Refer to your opening statement, and the main points. Remember to restate your main ideas. Reflect the logic of the argument, and show that your position is the supported one. (You might at this point want to go back to your first paragraph and edit it, so that the link between the introduction and the conclusion is clear.)
Bibliography	This is a list of the sources you consulted.
References	These are the sources from which you used ideas and/or quotes.

For advice on how to use persuasive language and rhetorical devices in your essay have a look at the table on pages 136–138 in Chapter 5 "Presentation Skills".

NOW...

Save, and print if possible. You have finished your draft. (Not your essay, yet!)

Have a break for a day or two, if there is time. If you do not have days to spare, then at least leave it for an hour or two.

Reviewing your persuasive/argumentative essay

Reread your essay, with a pencil in your hand to correct it. Give it to a friend to read.

Ask: "Does it make sense? Am I convinced by the argument? Will a reader understand the way I have presented my evidence, and agree with my argument?"

Edit, correct and rewrite as necessary. Ask your friend if they were convinced. If possible, give it to your teacher for review.

We can only improve by accepting and acting on constructive criticism. Once you have received feedback on your essay, go over it carefully, making sure that you really understand the comments. Use them as the basis for improvement next time. Think of the feedback as a friend tasting your cake—hopefully they will like it, but they may have recommendations that, if followed, will make you a superb cook!

After this, hand in your essay and relax. You have done a good job!

ANALYTICAL ESSAYS

During your school career you will be asked to write analytical essays in different subject areas such as languages and humanities, on a number of texts, both literary (novels, plays, poems) and non-literary (newspaper and magazine articles, speeches, leaflets, advertisements, etc). These essays may take a variety of forms, including:

- a literary response/commentary on a poem or prose extract
- an analytical essay on an aspect of a novel or play you have studied in class
- an analysis of a magazine or newspaper article
- an analysis of a print or television advertisement
- an analysis of a web page
- an analysis of a speech about a controversial issue.

In each case the purpose is to offer an informed interpretation of, and response to, the content and message of the text. No matter what type of text you are given, the basic elements you will be analysing are the same.

- The WHAT—the content and ideas being expressed; the author's message or purpose in writing the text
- The HOW—the linguistic and stylistic devices used by the writer
- The EFFECTS—on the reader of those linguistic and stylistic techniques

Thinking about your material

Whatever text you are analysing, it is important to know the text you are writing about well. This means reading it carefully, considering the following:

- its **context**—extract from a novel, poem from an anthology, article from a particular newspaper
- its **audience**—in terms of age, gender
- its **purpose**—the writer's intention to inform, persuade, entertain, cause you to reflect, convey a mood, memory or emotion, or something else
- its **content**—the main ideas in the piece; what is being said.

Then you need to look at the **techniques** (choices in language and style) used by the writer—how he or she has communicated their message. Finally, you need to consider and comment on the **effects** of the writer's linguistic and stylistic choices. See the diagram below.

AUDIENCE/PURPOSE/ CONTENT	LANGUAGE/STYLE	EFFECTS/IMPACT
Who is the text aimed at? *What is its purpose?* *What is the text about?* *What are the key points?*	*How is the text organized?* *What literary devices are used?* *What vocabulary is used?* *How is the text structured?*	*What effects are created by the language, linguistic and stylistic features?* *How are structure and layout used to reinforce the message?*

If you are writing about a novel you should first know the text well. You may have read the opinions of critics and listened to the ideas of your classmates or teacher but most important of all is to know what your own conclusions and opinions are, and to ensure you can support them with evidence from the text.

Planning your analytical essay

Let's take the example of a task you will probably be asked to complete during your course: writing a commentary or literary analysis of an extract from a text you are studying in class (poem, novel, drama or non-fiction text).

Step 1: Thinking about your ideas

A good strategy is to examine the text as if you were looking at it through a microscope. Read it carefully several times and on each occasion with a specific purpose. As you do so, shift your focus between the overall content, ideas and message of the text and the smaller details of language and style (diction, literary devices (alliteration, metaphors) structural features, etc). Switching between the broader focus on the bigger picture and the more microscopic focus on the linguistic and stylistic details of the text will help you make connections between the two. The aim is to always focus on HOW the language and style work to reinforce and help communicate the message (the WHAT) and ideas of the writer.

Annotating your text

As you read and reread the text, annotate it and make notes of your thoughts, reactions and observations. There are many different ways to annotate and make notes and the method(s) you choose will be those that suit your learning style best. The important thing to remember is to choose an approach that allows you to quickly and easily review and understand your notes. Some possible approaches you might use include:

- colour-coding—using colours here to highlight patterns of imagery, diction, structural features, etc
- underlining/circling/boxing the patterns using different variations of each
- making lists—you might choose to record the patterns you see as a list beside the text
- writing questions alongside the text
- writing comments or key words alongside the text.

You may find that in order to give you greater scope to track more things, you use a combination of these techniques.

At this stage you should also be thinking about which examples best illustrate your analysis.

Two Hands

My father in his study sits up late,
a pencil nodding stiffly in the hand
that thirteen times between breakfast and
supper led a scalpel an intricate
dance. The phone has sobbed itself to sleep
but he has articles to read. I curse
tonight, at the other end of the house,
this other hand whose indecisions keep
me cursing nightly; fingers with some style
on paper, elsewhere none. Who would have thought
hands so alike – spade palms, blunt fingers short
in the joint – would have no more in common? All
today, remembering the one, I have watched
the other save no one, serve no one, dance
with this pencil. Hand, you may have your chance
to stitch a life for fingers that have stitched
new life for many. Down the *Lancet** margin
this hand moves rapidly as mine moves slow.
A spasm shakes the phone at this elbow
The pencil drops: he will be out again

Jon Stallworthy,
Root and Branch (Phoenix Living Poets) (1976)

sibilants –
stillness, silence

sense of beauty
and art – admiration
of father's work

hands, confusing
to distinguish which
he is talking about

angry, resentful

sibilants –
frustration, silence

physical distance

Cursing.
Sense of
frustration at his
own work? Or at
lack of contact
with his
father?

negative view of
his own work and
worth in comparison
with father

central question

phone – personified

medical terms
Lancet,
scalpel,
stitch a life

pencil – both use
but one making notes,
son is creating poem.
Movement shows how
they work differenly

feels rejection?
Anger?

contrasts: the one/the other: saved 13 ppl/saved none; at different ends
of the house; moves rapidly, moves slow; indecision/sense of purpose

Lancet: medical journal

Step 2: Structuring your response

Once you have made notes on the features of the text outlined above, it is time to organize your ideas into a tightly structured argument that will provide a clear line of thought and persuade your reader that your analysis is credible and supported with clear evidence.

The structure of your analysis may vary depending on the type of text you are dealing with. For example, when writing a commentary on a poem, if there is a clearly logical development of ideas, you may follow the poem's structure, dealing with each stanza in turn. Alternatively, you may analyse the poem by looking at different features of style and language in separate paragraphs. However, whichever format you choose the basic ingredients of your essay sections will remain the same.

Introduction	Paragraph contextualizing text, outlining your thesis or argument—key ideas, the author's intention and message, point of view, tone and key techniques used to communicate that message plus your opinion on the strengths or weaknesses of the text.
Body paragraphs *Organized either as a holistic analysis of different features of style or language, or following the structure of the text (eg, stanza by stanza in a poem). This will vary according to the text being discussed*	Point outlining analysis of author's message, ideas and linguistic and stylistic techniques used to communicate them. Supporting evidence in the form of quotations and references integrated seamlessly into your paragraph. Detailed analysis of that evidence explaining how the language and style work to convey the writer's message and ideas. Summary sentence linking back to the topic sentence or thesis and, if relevant, looking ahead to the next point.
Conclusion	Summarize the most important point(s) of your analysis. Explain the main effect or impact of the text on the reader/viewer. Outline the main strengths of the text. Offer a personal response to the text in terms of the effectiveness of the writer's techniques in communicating his or her message. Comment.

Writing your analytical essay

Using your plan and notes you are now ready to begin writing your essay. Here is how you could go about it, focusing on one section at a time.

Introduction

The introduction of your essay previews what is to come. It is therefore important that you take time to clearly set out for your reader the main ideas of your analysis and the aspects you will be focusing on.

You may need to begin by contextualizing the extract before outlining the writer's intended purpose and message and highlighting the key features of language and style that enable him or her to communicate that message. You also need to explain the effect on the reader of those linguistic and stylistic choices.

Here is one possible format for an introduction. Remember, you will only have space and time to focus on the key points and ideas here.

CONTEXT: the WHERE	Explain the context of the piece. (If it is an extract for commentary, where does it occur in the text? What sort of publication is it taken from?)
CONTENT: the WHAT the WHY	Explain the writer's purpose in writing the text. Outline the main ideas—who, what, where, when, why—in as concise and detailed a manner as you can. Comment on the point of view and tone adapted by the writer.

> **TIPS**
>
> In particular when studying literary texts, which explore conflicts and tensions, look for shifts and changes in:
>
> - the situation, the action taking place and/or the relationship between characters
> - setting, mood or atmosphere
> - tone of the speaker—sarcastic, desperate, humorous, depressed.

APPROACH: the HOW writer's techniques and their effects	Explain the principle ways in which form, style and language choices reflect the author's intentions and ideas. Focus here on the KEY techniques only and their MAIN effects. These might include any of the following: • structural elements (line/sentence/stanza lengths, pace/flow of writing) • imagery/image patterns (similes, metaphors, allusions) • point of view • use of foreshadowing/flashback • diction—the type and texture of words • sound devices.

ACTIVITY

ATL Skills: organization, communication, thinking, reflection

Time: 20 minutes

Individual

SETTING OFF ON THE RIGHT FOOT

Examine the four introductions below analysing different types of texts to see how well they cover key elements of an introduction (context, purpose, content, viewpoint, tone, stylistic and linguistic choices and their effects). Then write an analytical introduction for this chapter in which you incorporate the key points you have learnt about essay writing and the main approaches and techniques outlined above, and say something about the way in which they have been presented and your own opinion on the advice given. Begin with the following sentence.

"Chapter 2 on essay writing ..."

Example 1: A commentary on a prose extract from *Lord of the Flies*

In this tense extract from Chapter 2, which describes how the boys' efforts to build a signal fire spiral out of control, Golding's aim is to explore the theme of human nature—in this case, their gradual descent into savagery—through descriptions of the fire and the conflict between Jack and Piggy that this arouses. This conflict, which in thematic terms is between the human extremes of reason and emotion, is explored through a range of techniques including the symbol of the fire itself, which reflects the shifting atmosphere and changes in the boys themselves, animal imagery and heated dialogue to emphasize the boys' emerging savage nature, and finally contrasts to highlight their different reactions to the fire. The tension in the passage builds as the conflict between Piggy, the adult voice of rational authority, struggles to be heard above the boys' increasing clamour.

Example 2: Analysis of a magazine article

In his article "The dangers of downloading music", published in the Music Monthly, *John Simms addresses the concerns of the music industry regarding illegal downloading of music from the internet, in particular his fear that music will eventually disappear if internet piracy continues eating away at the market. While he recognizes the potential benefits in terms of publicity and advertising for musicians, Simms' biased and negative view of human beings means he sees malicious intent where none is intended, exaggerating the potential damage to the industry while ignoring key benefits and opportunities that such access has brought to artists, producers and the public.*

Example 3: Analysis of an advertisement

This advertisement from the Royal Society for the Prevention of Cruelty to Animals (RSPCA) *focuses on persuading the public to support their calls for changes to the laws about the transportation of live animals. By using images and text portraying sheep being transported in cramped, unhygienic and inhumane conditions, the writer seeks to highlight the plight of many animals transported long distances in this manner. The writer directly captures the reader's attention by linking the animals' transportation to their final preparation as a meal, thus highlighting the huge contrast between the appeal of the meal and the terrible conditions they endure on the journey. Furthermore, through a blend of hard-hitting factual statements, ironic puns and emotive language, the writer produces a powerful and persuasive argument for changing the laws regarding live animal transportation.*

Example 4: Analysis of a poem

Carole Satyamurti's poem "Passed On" is both a nostalgic memorial to a dead mother and a celebration of independence told through an intimate first-person voice. Through the triple wordplay of the title, the metaphor of the box and cards, the italicized sections and the shifts in the voice and time, the writer explores the complex relationship between a mother and daughter before and after the mother's death. Furthermore, by adopting a shifting structure, syntax and sound imagery and setting the poem on a beach, the writer successfully conveys how the daughter finally breaks free of her mother's protective influence.

Body paragraphs

A common approach to paragraphing is the PEEL format.

> **P**oint—this should appear in your topic sentence.
>
> **E**vidence—include quotations or references to the text.
>
> **E**xplanation/evaluation of the evidence—explain effects of style/language choices.
>
> To make this a PEEL approach, you can also **L**ink the point back to your thesis or key argument(s) and, if relevant, the next point.

Point: Writing effective topic sentences

Topic sentences normally appear at, or near, the start of your paragraph and they tell the reader what your paragraph will be about. In an analytical essay they play a vital role in signalling the content and shape of your analysis. In a commentary or analytical response your **topic sentences** should highlight both the WHAT (the message) and the HOW (the **linguistic and stylistic techniques**) used to communicate that message.

Have a look at the examples below from different types of analytical tasks.

Through exaggerated and ironic descriptions of character X, the author creates a comic picture of him and undermines his credibility.

The car's image as a luxury vehicle is promoted through the use of comments from experts and persuasive adjectives.

The damage caused by illegal logging in the Amazon is highlighted by the writer's use of emotive language and shocking statistics.

A writing frame like this one for a literary analytical response can help you write good topic sentences.

Highlighting the role of the writer in this	Literary device/ linguistic or stylistic techniques (the HOW)	Verb to show its effect/functions		Idea/theme/ message/mood (the WHAT)
The writer's use of	symbolic setting	conveys	hints at	
	images of …	illustrates	symbolizes	
	detailed description of …	shows	connotes	
	the symbols of …	signifies	highlights	
	contrasts in …	reflects	emphasizes	
	changes in …	implies	reinforces	
	sounds	suggests	underlines	
	(repeated) references to …	demonstrates	underscores	

It is even better if you can also highlight in the topic sentence **the effects** of the linguistic and stylistic features used by the writer. Have a look at the example below.

TECHNIQUE (HOW)   **THEME (WHAT)**

By setting the scene solely in Nora's house, Ibsen highlights her sense of entrapment and allows the audience to experience the suffocating atmosphere of marriage.

EFFECT

Use the writing frame to help you practise how to do this.

Writer's role	The device (HOW)	Use/function	The WHAT	Verb expressing communication	Evidence
The writer's use of	Imagery/sounds/ contrasts, etc	to convey/to show/to reflect/ to illustrate, etc	A theme, idea, attitude relationship, etc	is evident/seen/ highlighted, etc	in the references to x as " … "

Point: Thinking about the focus of your topic sentences

Another key point to consider as you construct your topic sentences is what aspect you wish to make your reader focus on. Considering the three sentences we looked at earlier, the first focuses on the writer's techniques (*exaggerated and ironic descriptions of character X*)—the HOW—while the second and third focus on the idea being communicated (*"The car's image as a luxury vehicle"* and *"The damage caused by illegal logging"*)—the WHAT. Varying the focus of your sentences will also add variety and interest for your reader. To look at this in a little more detail, decide whether the primary focus of your paragraph will be on a) the WHAT—the writer's intentions and message, or b) the HOW—the writer's techniques.

Point: Using transitions/discourse markers

Transitions or discourse markers help the reader follow your arguments clearly. They are like the signposts directing the reader on their journey through your response. They should signal the direction of your analysis—whether you are continuing a line of argument or changing to look at a counter-argument or interpretation. Below is a list of common transitions/discourse markers.

Compare/contrast	Same point (and/also)	But	To sum up/so
Unlike x, y …	In addition, …	However, …	In conclusion, …
Like x, y …	Similarly, …	Nonetheless, …	In summary, …
While x …, y …	Furthermore, …	Nevertheless, …	Thus, …
On the one hand … while on the other hand …	Not only … but also …	Despite this, …	Therefore, …
Whereas x …, y …		Even so, …	Clearly then, …
X …, whereas y …			

Remember, you can vary the position of the transition/discourse marker by placing it at the start of your topic sentence (where it adds more emphasis) or embedding it within the sentence, as in the examples below.

- *To **further** highlight the boys' descent into savagery, Golding …*
- *The writer **also** creates antipathy towards the fashion industry by …*
- *There are, **however**, numerous …*

THINKING ABOUT THE FOCUS OF YOUR SENTENCES

1. Using a table like the one below, sort the sentences by whether they foreground the techniques or the author's intentions. (The first two have been done for you.)
   - Golding's use of animal imagery to portray the boys as savage creates antipathy towards …
   - The negative effects of whaling are highlighted through comments from Greenpeace …
   - The repetition of "We can end this now!" in the third paragraph of the speech reinforces …
   - The distance between the father and son is underscored in the poem's final line where …
   - The stilted sentencing and frequent pauses in the speech create …
   - The writer highlights the dangers of driving while using mobile phones by …
   - The evocative image of the crying baby creates sympathy and outrage in the reader …
   - Through a regular rhyme and rhythm the poet emphasizes the monotonous motion of the …
   - A sense of disorientation in the speaker is evoked through words such as "dizzy" and …
   - Ivan's fear and doubt are emphasized through his repeated questions to his team leader …

Sentences foregrounding techniques (the HOW)	Sentences foregrounding the content, message and/or author's intentions (the WHAT)
• *Golding's use of animal imagery to portray the boys as savage …*	• *The negative effects of whaling are highlighted …*

2. Using a recent piece of your own analytical writing try rewriting the topic sentence, focusing on varying between emphasizing the techniques or the intentions and ideas being communicated.

Evidence: Incorporating quotations or references to the text

> **P**oint—this should appear in your topic sentence.
>
> **E**vidence—include quotations or references to the text.
>
> **E**xplanation/evaluation of the evidence—explain effects of style/language.
>
> To make this a PEEL approach, you can also **L**ink the point back to your thesis or key argument(s) and, if relevant, the next point.

In order to make your analysis convincing to an examiner you must support your ideas with well-chosen evidence from the text. This is the key to scoring high marks! Quotations should be short, seamlessly integrated and well chosen. Students sometimes have problems embedding quotations effectively in their writing. Here are some guidelines that may help you.

Example

Your point:	The island is personified as a living breathing monster.
Your quotation:	"The sea breathed again in a long slow sigh."

You need to introduce the quotation correctly and also make sure it makes SENSE grammatically in your writing.

For example: *The island's personification as "a living breathing monster" is compounded in Golding's description of how the sea "breathed again in a long slow sigh".*

Note: Pick out the key words/phrase from the quotation. Avoid copying it all.

You may need to adjust your sentence so that the quotation makes grammatical sense within it. However, sometimes this is difficult. For example, if the tense of the quotation is different from your present-tense commentary you can change the quotation using square brackets and putting your change in the brackets.

For example: *"The conch is utterly destroyed as it "explode[s] into a thousand white fragments and cease[s] to exist"* (Golding: 54).

Sometimes you may wish to omit certain words from a sentence or a phrase that you wish to quote. To do this you could use an ellipsis (a set of three dots . . .)

Remembering these key points will help you.

- Keep quotations short—between two and five words is often best. The key is to select the main words/phrases and focus on these, rather than copying out whole sentences.
- Avoid using a quotation that merely repeats or paraphrases your own words.
- Embed/integrate your quotations within your paragraph so they make sense.
- Copy the quotation exactly as it appears in the original; if you alter any words use [ ] or if you miss words out use an ellipsis (a set of three dots . . .).
- Reference your quotations (chapter/page/line number). Add a bibliography at the end showing which edition you have used.

The writing frame below is one way of introducing quotations into your literary response.

The description of x as "——" By describing x as "—" (and "—") *author's name*	signifies/reflects/implies/suggests/ hints at/symbolizes/connotes/ highlights/emphasizes	put the effect/impact on the reader here

A final word about accuracy. It is very important that you copy quotations exactly as they appear in the original text. Think of your evidence as something to be presented in court. Changing or tampering with the original invalidates it in a courtroom and will not impress a judge. Your examiner will not be impressed if you present quotations inaccurately.

Evidence: Referencing your quotations

If you quote from a text or an extract be sure to include the line or page number of the text. This is helpful for an examiner if they want to refer to a reference you have made to the text in order to check its accuracy and/or location.

ACTIVITY

ATL Skills: communication, reflection, thinking, transfer

 Time: 15 minutes

 Class

REVIEWING THE USE OF EVIDENCE IN YOUR ANALYTICAL ESSAYS

Reread a recent analytical essay you have written and annotate it as follows.

1. Read each paragraph carefully and alongside it write the letter "G" or "E" in the margin. "G" stands for paragraphs that make general statements about the passage/work without any supporting evidence, while "E" stands for paragraphs that provide evidence for specific points. There should be more "E" than "G" paragraphs.
2. Highlight the **quotations/text references** in each paragraph you labelled with the letter "E". Check they are short, embedded seamlessly and referenced.
3. In a different colour highlight the explanation of **the effects** of language and style.
4. Now read the topic sentences. These should be linked so there is logic in your answer. Highlight the **transitions** with a new colour.

Practising this sort of review activity will help you write better analytical essays.

Explaining and evaluating the evidence

Point—this should appear in your topic sentence.

Evidence—include quotations or references to the text.

Explanation/evaluation of the evidence—explain effects of style/language choices.

To make this a PEEL approach, you can also **L**ink the point back to your thesis or key argument(s) and, if relevant, the next point.

The most important part of your paragraph is your analysis and explanation of the evidence you present. This is where you score most of your marks and show the examiner that you can explain the writer's use of language for a particular effect and evaluate its impact on a reader. You should try to comment on individual words and phrases in the evidence/quotation you use within your paragraph. Below is an example from an analysis of an article on deforestation in the Amazon rainforest.

The writer creates antipathy towards the logging companies through alliteration of the words "destructive", "damaging" and "deforestation", which creates a clear negative connection between their activities and the impact on the Amazon Basin.

Below are some useful phrases to introduce your explanation and evaluation of the evidence.

- The description of x as "＿＿" and "＿＿" implies …
- The reference to x as "＿＿" and "＿＿" conveys …
- The depiction of x as "＿＿" …
- The portrayal of x as seen in references to her as "＿＿" and "＿＿" suggests …
- The terms "x", "y" and "z" all emphasize the extent to which …
- The phrase "＿＿" …
- The word "＿＿" …
- The sentence "＿＿＿＿＿" …
- The line "＿＿＿＿＿" conveys …
- In the words of x: "＿＿＿" …
- By using the term "＿＿" the author …
- The personification of x as "＿＿" …

When commenting on the effects of language and style, look at the nature, type and impact of words chosen by the writer, the images, associations and impressions they create in the reader's mind. To help you review, the list of devices and their effects is on pages 136–138.

TIPS

Linking your essay to a modern context or your own personal experience shows you are **engaging** with the material and considering it in relation to your own situation. Has the title or the topic made you think about your own life and the society you are a member of?

Example

In using repeated references to stillness and silence to highlight his characters' increasing sense of loneliness and loss, Steinbeck touches on a common human experience. In an increasingly alienating high-tech world, we spend too little time pausing to reflect on the value of friendship or to contemplate what we have lost. Steinbeck's motif draws attention to this and evokes sympathy for his lonely characters.

Writing conclusions

Writing good conclusions is an art and involves practice and thought. It is the final word and, therefore, crucial in leaving your audience with the feeling they have been convinced (or not) by your ideas and interpretation.

In your conclusion you should **avoid**:

- merely repeating all your arguments
- ending with a direct question.

Instead, try to **ensure** you:

1. address the question directly and answer it
2. summarize your most powerful arguments without repeating them all
3. offer a personal engagement with the topic/theme/issue
4. make an impact on your reader and leave him or her thinking.

Have a look at the example on the left from an analytical essay on the motif of silence and stillness in *Of Mice and Men*.

Reviewing your analytical essay

Having completed your essay it is important that you read it through again to check both your ideas and your expression. Proofreading your work can save you valuable marks. If you are given a timed assessment be sure you leave five minutes at the end for proofreading and checking your work. It will earn you valuable marks. In particular, you should ensure that your response:

- has a clear line of thought and a logical structure ☐
- uses transitions and discourse markers to guide the reader through the essay ☐
- incorporates evidence from the text that is copied accurately and referenced appropriately ☐
- examines the effects of the writer's linguistic and stylistic choices ☐
- uses an appropriately formal vocabulary and tone. ☐

Considering your language

You may have found that during the drafting stage you focused more on the content of your response than on the language you used. The reviewing stage is a good opportunity to now carefully check your language. In addition to other aspects of language discussed earlier, here are a list of things you could look at in terms of appropriate language for an analytical essay.

Have you used the present tense?

When analysing a text, it is important to make sure you write in the present tense.

Have you avoided using informal, chatty, "spoken" language in your writing?

- Avoid contractions such as "isn't", "don't", "couldn't", etc.
- Avoid using "you" or "we" when talking about the reader or "I" when referring to your own response. Adopting a more impersonal tone will make your analysis sound more formal, objective and considered.

Have you focused on your verbs?

Your verbs are important in signalling to the examiner the effect of the writer's techniques that you are analysing. Below are some useful verbs you could incorporate in your writing.

Verbs signalling emphasis	highlights, reinforces, underlines, underscores, accentuates, foregrounds
Verbs signalling illustration	conveys, illustrates, shows, exemplifies, demonstrates, indicates
Verbs explaining meaning	connotes, symbolizes, signifies, implies, reflects, infers, suggests, evokes

Have you used technical language appropriate to your analysis?

For example, for a literary essay you may use terms such as those mentioned below. Can you add to the list?

Sound devices	alliteration, assonance, euphony, cacophony, rhyme, onomatopoeia
Imagery	symbol, image, motif, allusion, simile, metaphor, personification
Structural devices	enjambment, caesura, end-stopped lines, line break, repetition, anaphora
Other	hyperbole, understatement, diction, meter, rhyme

Have you used precise adjectives?

Remember to use adjectives or modifiers when exploring a writer's techniques. These help you to be more precise in your analysis of a writer's techniques and their effects and will give the examiner the impression that you are thinking carefully about the choices made by the writer. Look at the examples below from a commentary on a poem.

a … tone	contemplative, reflective, ironic, tender, intimate, impersonal, confessional
… images (of …)	powerful, vivid, disturbing, shocking, natural, contrasting
a … structure	regular, irregular, shifting
a … pace	fast, frantic, moderate, slow, lumbering, cumbersome
… textured words	coarse, smooth, soft, harsh
makes a … impact	dramatic, understated, impersonal, shocking, disturbing

Have you presented your ideas in a concise manner?

One of the skills when writing an analytical essay is condensing your ideas into a short space. You may even be given a word limit. In order to help you write more concisely, you need to learn to nominalize when you write. This means turning verbs and adjectives and other groups of words into nouns and noun groups. Converting them into nouns and noun groups allows you to comment on them as an entity or thing and add information to your sentences and clauses. Look, for example, at the following extracts from students' analytical responses.

a) *The poem has no regular structure and this reflects how the speaker's life is chaotic.*

   becomes

   The lack of a regular structure reflecting the chaos of the speaker's life …

b) *The writer shows how the character grows more and more isolated by describing how he starts taking long walks on his own.*

becomes

The depiction of the character's increasing isolation in descriptions of his long solitary walks …

c) *The article states that there are rising numbers of accidents because more and more people are driving their cars while using their mobile phones. The writer comments in paragraph two that this is both "irresponsible" and "dangerous".*

becomes

The cause of the rise in accidents, attributed to an increase in the use of mobile phones among drivers, is described in paragraph two as "irresponsible" and "dangerous".

d) *The speaker criticizes the logging companies for failing to compensate the local tribes. This is shown when he refers to them as "greedy" and "uncaring".*

becomes

The speaker's criticism of the logging companies' failure to compensate local tribes, evident in his references to them as "greedy" and "uncaring" …

The underlined words and phrases that are nominalized (turned into noun groups) allow the writer to pack more information into each clause and so extend the density of information in each sentence. In c) and d) two sentences are condensed into one, and in a) and b) the writer has the freedom to continue the sentence by including a piece of evidence or a comment on the effect of the writer's choices.

You are now ready to submit your essay! Remember, with practice you will become more skilled in using these strategies and will be able to work more efficiently through the stages of the task.

KEY POINTS OF THE CHAPTER

ATL skills of essay-writing

- Organization
- Information literacy
- Communication
- Thinking
- Transfer
- Reflection

The two most important things to remember are to manage your time effectively and to maintain academic honesty.

The four main stages of essay-writing

- Organizing the material
- Planning the essay
- Writing the essay
- Reviewing the essay

The three main types of essay examined in this chapter

- Narrative/descriptive essays
- Persuasive/argumentative essays
- Analytical essays

Finally, you can learn to do this! Good essay writers are made, not born.

Useful websites

http://www2.actden.com/writ_den/tips/essay/index.htm. This is a very simple site that takes you through the steps of writing several different kinds of essays.

http://www.brainpop.com/english/. This site has some free materials. For others you will need to pay a small subscription. It is worth it, as their characters, Tim and Moby, take you through the essentials of writing an essay using animated videos that are easy to understand.

http://www.britannica.com/

http://www.easybib.com. This is a free site that will allow you to automatically create references in the format you choose.

http://www.eric.ed.gov

http://www.factmonster.com

http://freeology.com/graphicorgs/. This has all types of graphic organizers.

http://www.internet4classrooms.com/assessment_assistance/assessment_preparation_language_arts_topic_sentence.htm

http://netforbeginners.about.com/od/navigatingthenet/tp/top_10_search_engines_for_beginners.htm

http://www.readwritethink.org/files/resources/interactives/persuasion_map/

http://www.timeforkids.com/TFK/media/hh/pdfs/ideaorganizers/persuasive_ideaorg.pdf

http://www.youtube.com/watch?v=DwDVmBDgubw&feature=results_main&playnext=1&list=PL784FF9616E9DE1B4

http://www.youtube.com/watch?v=13NYEimqla8&feature=BFa&list=PL784FF9616E9DE1B4&lf=results_main

References

International Baccalaureate. 2008. *MYP: From principles into practice.* Cardiff, UK. International Baccalaureate Organization.

Steinbeck, J. 1952. *East of Eden.* New York, USA. Viking.

In this chapter you will learn:

- how to use the design cycle effectively and successfully
- which ATL skills will support you in using the design cycle
- the importance of academic honesty and time management
- how to interpret primary resources
- how to put theory into practice.

All creative processes in technology begin with a problem or a perceived need. The design cycle, when used in partnership with ATL, is a great tool to help you to put your ideas into practice.

"You start with nothing and try not to ruin it."
Gary Hume

"Ideas are fragile."
Jonathan Ive

"Most people make the mistake of thinking design is what it looks like. People think it's this veneer—that the designers are handed this box and told, 'Make it look good!' That's not what we think design is. It's not just what it looks like and feels like. Design is how it works."
Steve Jobs

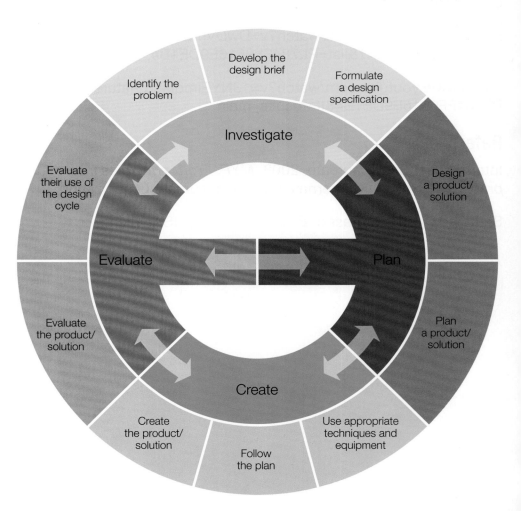

Investigate
- Identify the problem
- Develop the design brief
- Formulate a design specification

Plan
- Design a product/solution
- Plan a product/solution
- Use appropriate techniques and equipment

Create
- Follow the plan
- Create the product/solution

Evaluate
- Evaluate the product/solution
- Evaluate their use of the design cycle

> *"There's a misconception that invention is about having a great idea, tinkering with it in the garden shed for a few days, then appearing with the finished design. In fact, it's a far longer and iterative process—trying something over and over, changing one small variable at a time. Trial and error."*
>
> James Dyson

Iterative: Repeating a process with the aim of approaching a desired result.

Jonathan Ive, James Dyson and Steve Jobs are three of the most influential designers of the 21st century and have shown us how, in order to design well, we need to follow good, established design principles.

Although products such as the Dyson vacuum cleaner or the iPad may be designed and manufactured with ease of use in mind, the design process itself is far from easy and requires careful planning and perseverance. In this chapter, the skills you learn will be invaluable for completing multiple projects, not just in technology.

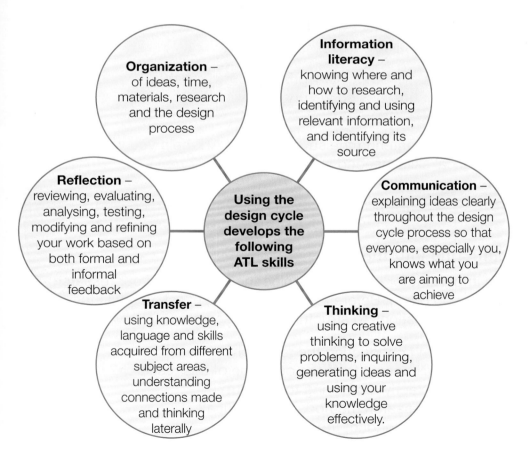

Organization – of ideas, time, materials, research and the design process

Information literacy – knowing where and how to research, identifying and using relevant information, and identifying its source

Reflection – reviewing, evaluating, analysing, testing, modifying and refining your work based on both formal and informal feedback

Using the design cycle develops the following ATL skills

Communication – explaining ideas clearly throughout the design cycle process so that everyone, especially you, knows what you are aiming to achieve

Transfer – using knowledge, language and skills acquired from different subject areas, understanding connections made and thinking laterally

Thinking – using creative thinking to solve problems, inquiring, generating ideas and using your knowledge effectively.

To think laterally: Thinking in a creative way to try to solve problems.

Now let's take a look at the different stages of the design cycle in more detail.

INVESTIGATE

The investigate stage of the design cycle provides the foundation for problem-solving. Being able to identify and extract relevant information from a range of sources is a very important skill. Also remember that the solution to the problem you are investigating may result in some benefit for society, the environment or even the world!

ACTIVITY

ATL skills: information literacy, collaboration reflection, organization, transfer

 Time: 15 minutes

 Individual

TEN PRINCIPLES OF DESIGN

Search on the internet for Dieter Rams' "10 principles of good design".

Using the seven ATL skills as a guide, write as many skills as possible that you think you would need in order to fulfill these 10 design principles.

Using Rams' "good design" principles, write down 10 possible principles of **bad** design in your own words.

How can mastering the seven skills of ATL help you with the practical skills needed in MYP technology?

Gathering information

It is important for you to determine the purpose of your research before you begin. Before asking anyone else, ask yourself the following questions to structure your research.

- **Why** am I conducting the research?
- **Who** will benefit from the outcome of this research?
- **What** exactly am I trying to find out?
- **Which** research methods should I use?
- **How** will I conduct the research?
- **When** and **where** will I be conducting the research?

A reliable researcher will use a variety of sources for their project and the following sections contain tips to help you become an effective investigator.

Identifying reliable primary and secondary sources

A **primary** source of information is collected by the individual who is going to use it. It requires first-hand interpretation using all five senses—sound, vision, touch, taste and smell. Primary sources include:

- an analysis of artifacts, objects and products
- an analysis of research notes or design patents
- conducting interviews
- carrying out trials.

A **secondary** source of information is collected by others so it requires second-hand interpretation. Secondary sources include:

- a history textbook
- stories
- anthropometric data
- websites
- films
- biographies.

web links

Here are several websites specifically for design that you may find useful as a secondary source.

The Design Museum: http://designmuseum.org/.

The Craft Council: http://www.craftscouncil.org.uk/.

Victoria and Albert Museum: http://www.vam.ac.uk/.

Dyson: http://www.dyson.co.uk/.

TIPS

When researching for any project, try to use a combination of primary and secondary sources to support and balance your argument.

In the example below, a student is trying to assess the benefits of good computer design. They have decided to look at the history of Apple computers and have researched an early example on display at the Science Museum in London.

What is being investigated?	Key observations using primary sources	Key observations using secondary sources	Questions about the product
• The Apple II microcomputer (1977) and some information about it on display at the Science Museum in London	• Plastic case • Able to display text and graphics in colour • Two floppy disk inputs, similar size to CDs • Rainbow Apple logo on the packaging • Small screen compared to modern computers	• Designed and built by Steve Jobs and Steve Wozniak by the end of 1976 • First mass-market personal computer	• How does the Apple design differ from other computers produced at the time? • What need was it fulfilling that no others did? • What happened around 1977 that might indicate why there was a need for it? • Are there any clues in this early model about the future design of Apple computers?

TIPS

In any investigation, it's important to acknowledge how bias can affect your research and the importance of keeping balance in your project.

WEBSITE COMPARISON

Using either hard copy or online sources, compare several reviews of a consumer product or solution. Here are some examples you might want to consider.

- 3D printer
- MP3 player
- Limbo-dancing robot

Firstly, use the following code to rate the sources of the reviews that you find.

Red—steer clear of, no use at all.
Amber—quite useful in parts but lacking in others.
Green—excellent, very thorough and highly recommended.

To help you come to this conclusion, analyse the sources you collect using the following questions.

- Is the website or publication known for being credible? For example, *Which?* (an online and print magazine available worldwide) could be seen as a reliable source.
- Does the layout look professional? Although this is not necessarily an indication of reliability or lack of bias, referring to poorly edited sources full of grammatical and spelling errors can undermine your research.
- Is the information accurate? Does the source use correctly cited material and acknowledgments? You have to cite and acknowledge your sources and it is no different for the professionals!
- Can you find similar information in other sources? Cross-check to verify information.
- Would you recommend the source to others? Talk to your peers about sites that they have found useful and reliable.
- How biased is the source? For example, are websites sponsored by advertisers? Think about garish advertising pop-ups appearing when you are using particular websites.

The more research that you carry out, the more you will develop an instinct for reliable sources.

ACTIVITY

ATL skills: communication, information literacy, organization, thinking, transfer

Time: 1 hour

Small groups

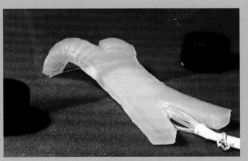

Questionnaires and surveys

Results from a questionnaire or a survey are an excellent source of material you can use as part of your research. In order to collect useful responses you need to be discerning in the questions you write.

The aim of good questions is to provide accurate and complete information from your respondents. This requires careful thought about the wording of questions. You can use the table below to help you.

Tips	Clarification	Unclear question	Clearer question
Avoid jargon and clarify terms.	*Your language should be clear to everyone, even second language learners.*	*Do you rely on cramming to do well in tests and exams?* ( ) yes ( ) no	*Do you rely on last minute intensive study to do well in tests and exams?* ( ) yes ( ) no
Avoid ambiguous questions and require precise answers.	*Avoid phrases like "how often", "how regularly", "how long" as people interpret these differently.*	*How long do you spend on homework?*	*On average, how many hours do you spend each week doing homework?* 0–2 3–5 6–8 9–11 12–14 15+
Avoid multiple questions.	*Ask for one piece of information at a time.*	*Do you watch television or listen to music when you study?* ( ) yes ( ) no	*Do you watch television when you study?* ( ) yes ( ) no *Do you listen to music when you study?* ( ) yes ( ) no
Avoid leading questions.	*Avoid phrases like such as "Would you agree that …" "Is it fair to say that …".*	*Do you think a quiet environment is important for effective study?* ( ) yes ( ) no ( ) no opinion	*How important is a quiet environment for effective study?* ( ) very important ( ) important ( ) quite important ( ) not important at all
Ensure options are mutually exclusive and cover sufficient ranges.	*Be sure there is only one possible answer for choices and that your options cover the full range of answers.* *If ranking statements clarify if 1 = highest or lowest.*	*How many hours, on average, do you spend doing homework each night?* <1 1–2 2–3	*How many hours, on average, do you spend doing homework each night?* 0–1 2–3 4–5 6 or more
Avoid (double) negatives.	*Phrase questions so they avoid negatives or double negatives.*	*Are you good at not being distracted by music when you study?* ( ) yes ( ) no ( ) no opinion	*Does music distract you when you study?* ( ) yes ( ) no

Academic honesty in more detail

> *"It takes less time to do a thing right than it does to explain why you did it wrong."*
> Henry Wadsworth Longfellow

Academic honesty will come up again and again throughout this book and in your classes. It might seem like teachers mention it too often but the consequences of not being academically honest are severe.

WHY ARE YOU IN SCHOOL?	To learn. To know. To speak your own mind.
WHY DOES INTEGRITY MATTER?	Integrity cultivates a reputation for being trustworthy and fair. IB students are principled and act with honesty and respect.
WHAT IS PLAGIARISM?	Representing the ideas or work of others as your own. Copying the work of others. A breach of academic integrity.
WHY IS PLAGIARISM WRONG?	It undermines your own integrity and the integrity of your school. It interferes with learning and creativity. It is unethical—and unfair.
HOW CAN YOU AVOID PLAGIARISM?	Quote accurately. Cite sources appropriately. Respect others' academic endeavours.

ARE YOU A CONTENT CREATOR?	Don't be a content imitator—let your own ideas take flight!
HOW CAN YOU HELP OTHERS?	Model honest behaviour. Don't let others copy your work. Work independently on independent assignments. Be sure the work you turn in is your own.
TRULY EARN YOUR GRADE!	Integrity is doing what is right—even when it is difficult.

TIPS

Make a point of reviewing your project regularly. Scan it for accuracy of information and the way you have presented this information. Have you kept track of every source used so that it can be used in your list of citations?

Your school will have consequences for students found guilty of academic malpractice. Remember, if you use more than 30 words taken from a source **without attribution** this is plagiarism. Get into the right habits now—the consequences are serious and potentially life changing.

Acknowledging that the idea is not your own, and allowing the reader to identify the original text from which it is taken, requires citing the source. For example:

In a study of innovative design (Jones, 2009, p 22) it was stated that the "MYP design cycle is wonderful".

An example of using an in-text reference correctly is as follows.

In Marianne Barrucand and Achim Bednorz's authoritative study of Moorish architecture in Andalusia, first published in 1992, …

You must then give the full reference to this text in the bibliography at the end of your project.

Barrucand, M and Bednorz, A. 2007. *Moorish Architecture in Andalusia*. 25th Anniversary/Icons Series. Cologne, Germany. Taschen.

Every source used must be identified and acknowledged. All acknowledged sources should be used to support other people's ideas. Microsoft Word can help you with this.

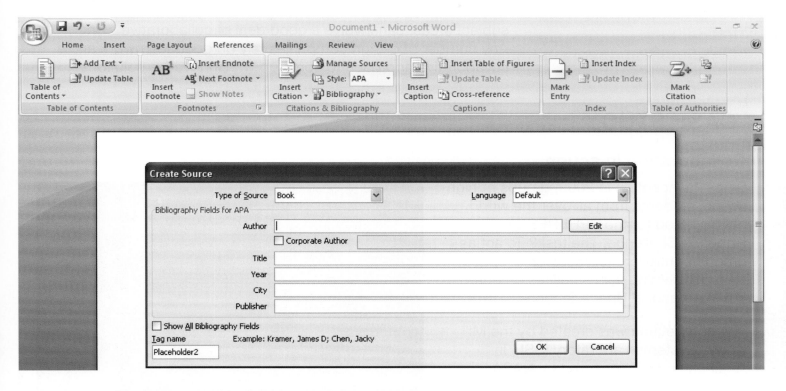

If you use any material not created by you, the source must be acknowledged. This material can include, but is not limited to:

- images—photos, cartoons, artwork, illustrations and drawings
- maps
- books, magazines and newspapers
- films and TV programmes
- letters
- journals
- computer programs
- blogs, websites and emails
- other people's ideas
- data graphs.

web links

Try http://www.evernote.com, an online resource that can help you to keep track of web research.

Investigating as part of a group

Where two or three or even four heads are better than one!

Creative problem-solving, not only for design projects but in many subject areas, can involve a good deal of collaborative work. Any number of design companies rely on good teamwork and a collaborative approach to come up with innovative solutions.

ATL skill: collaboration

CASE STUDY

Collaboration in action

Since its inception in 2009, groups of high school students from all over the world have applied for the SPHERES-Zero-Robotics Challenge. The task? To act as ground controllers for research in space by programming mini satellites on board the International Space Station.

The competition was created by the MIT Space Systems Laboratory (SSL) in America and is sponsored by NASA.

During the competition, each team must complete a set of predetermined tasks. During all phases, the students are challenged not only with programming, but also with the development of documentation and presentations to add to their engineering and communication skills. In all cases, the students have to learn and practise successful teamwork skills as there are minimum team size requirements.

web links

 Visit http://www.zerorobotics.org for more information.

GROUP WORK VERSUS COLLABORATION

Answer the first two questions on your own and then answer the third question as part of a group.

1. What skills do you think you need to be a good collaborator?
2. What skills do you think you need to be a good group worker?
3. What are the differences between group work and collaboration?

ACTIVITY

ATL skills: thinking

Time: 5 minutes

Individual and group

Demonstrating teamwork

Collaboration will reinforce social skills and help you to become a better communicator. Teamwork is a transferable skill that will serve you well throughout your school career, into further and higher education, and the world of work.

ATL skills: collaboration

ACTIVITY

ACTIVITY

ATL skills: collaboration

 Time: 20 minutes

  Group or Individual

ACTIONS FOR EFFECTIVE GROUP WORK

Copy the table below and add as many ideas as you can to each of the columns. The examples have been done for you.

The benefits of group work	The challenges of group work	Actions I can take for effective group working
Example: People from different backgrounds can bring a variety of different experiences and skills to the discussion.	**Examples:** Sometimes it feels as though not everyone has enough time to talk, and some people get left out. Big groups can mean that too many ideas are suggested and you might run out of time. Differences of opinion can cause conflict.	**Examples:** Agree on the **outcome** you would all like to achieve at the beginning of the discussion and keep referring to this if you get off track. Be prepared to change your opinion! You might have to.

Share your findings with the class and combine all of your "actions for effective group work" into a list.

TIPS

Academic honesty is an important consideration when collaborating. Remember to clearly identify your own work and the work of others in the team.

PLAN

These are the key design cycle components:

- design a product/solution
- plan a product/solution.

Don't underestimate the importance of planning and how it will benefit your project. The design cycle is a framework within which to operate. Use it!

Your planning will depend on the nature of the problem you have identified and the time you have to complete it. Planning, together with organization (an ATL skill area), is key for almost every project you undertake in your school career.

Here is how you can become an effective planner.

It is very important that you have a clear grasp of what is required of you. One of the most common mistakes made by students is to respond to the question or task they **think** they are being given rather than what is actually required.

There are sometimes several answers to a single problem, and several ways of answering a design brief.

Creating both ideas and concepts requires good thinking skills. Try working in groups of two or three to "bounce" initial ideas off each other. Collaboration often helps to clarify, even in the initial stages of a project, which ideas might be better than others. It will also help you to keep an open mind!

TIPS

ACTIVITY

ATL skills: thinking, transfer, communication

 Time: 20 minutes

 Individual

CHOOSING THE BEST SOLUTION

The James Dyson Award (http://www.jamesdysonaward.org) is an international competition for students of product design, engineering or industrial design. The requirement for the competition is to "design something that solves a problem".

In this activity, you will be discussing three different products that solve the same problem. You will first need to make a list of pros and cons for all three so that you can narrow down what is going to be the most effective solution. This exercise will require you to use your thinking skills to make good judgments about the relative merits of all three designs.

Pros			
Cons			

A SWOT analysis is a great way of testing your thinking. Choose a design of corkscrew and complete the following table.

Strengths	Weaknesses
Opportunities	**Threats**

Always use your research! This is the best way of being able to justify the decisions you make.

TIPS

85

Developing your ideas

Don't underestimate the importance of considering different alternatives; this is all part of the design process. However, for this to work, an essential part of the design cycle is being able to modify ideas based on what works—not just sticking to one approach.

Creating novel solutions

Good thinking skills will allow you to review, modify and refine your solution both during the planning stages and the actual creating process. Thinking skills during the design cycle process will also enable you to be both critical and analytical of what you are doing. James Dyson's design heroes are ones that have gone through a rigorous design process, often ending in failure. You have to be prepared for your design not to work! Dyson says: "Most people think testing is all about durability and reliability. Of course that's a big part of it. But before that happens … you need an idea that works. Dyson Engineers get those ideas often by trying the ridiculous. Most of the time it ends in failure. That's good. Failure sparks thinking and the extraordinary."

web links

Search YouTube for 'James Dyson Foundation on Teachers TV' to watch a video of students working in groups.

http://www.youtube.com/watch?v=tUTzeEl4yUc

Be prepared to take risks. Here is a brief guide in helping you to think outside the box.

- Do your design ideas inspire you? If not, it's probable that they might not inspire anyone else.
- Are you playing it safe? Think about design that inspires you. How does it stand out in terms of both form and function?
- The designer Thomas Edison said, "I have not failed. I've just found 10,000 ways that won't work." Have you tried an array of design ideas?
- Do your ideas come from a range of both primary and secondary sources? How have these informed your ideas and judgments?
- Don't think for one moment that if someone says your idea is "weird" it is a sign of bad design. Some of the strangest designs are perhaps some of the very best.

Managing your project

Time

It's easy for time to slip away. Make sure you schedule time and develop methods to meet all commitments for the project brief. Stick to deadlines and be realistic about what is achievable over a period of time. If you know that you work best between 6 o'clock and 7 o'clock in the evening, for instance, do your work then. Plan your schedule to ensure that you have your work and extra-curricular commitments in balance. This is not always easy— but, nevertheless, it can be done. By short-, mid- and long-term planning, you can identify where pressure points might be in terms of coursework deadlines. The best design projects begin with a solid timeline.

You can use a modified version of the study timetable on page 160 for all your major assignments.

Managing yourself might be the greatest challenge of all. Working effectively is all about being honest and, on occasion, critical of your working methods. Managing yourself isn't about yet another layer of stuff to do—it's all about effective working and ensuring success, but not to the detriment of your health and well-being. Don't worry, you won't be the only one who is managing a lot of different commitments.

Transferring your planning skills

The planning stage of the design cycle can be used in other subject areas. Good planning, in any subject area, will enable you to use the design cycle as well as the inquiry cycle, along with a whole range of planning strategies such as graphic organizers, mindmapping and class discussion. Skills acquired when using the design cycle will also enable you to:

- put your thoughts into logical order
- identify problems, and
- develop creative solutions in order to solve them.

One of the most important aspects of planning in the design cycle is to enable you to be critical about the information you have gathered and to consider multiple perspectives on an issue—so that you can test what the most successful and effective outcomes are going to be.

TIPS

Following a plan doesn't mean that you have to forget really good ideas. In fact, it could help them. Deal with the important information first and always really scrutinize your brief; take into account what is being asked of you.

Always save and back up your work! This saves heartache, stress, embarrassment, rage, etc!

ATL skills: thinking, transfer and communication, organization, reflection

CREATE

The key design cycle components are:

- follow the plan
- use appropriate techniques and equipment
- create the product/solution.

Creating your final design or product will require you to use the investigation and planning stages you have completed. It is important that you allow yourself time to make and create a suitable end product that demonstrates your grasp of the design cycle. If you have followed your plan and are using appropriate techniques and equipment, the result should be successful.

Here are some tips for the effective creation of a product or a solution. Taking a thoughtful approach to problem-solving when creating your product should enhance the final outcome and demonstrate how you have made your thoughts visible.

Justifying any changes to the plan

It is not the end of the world if you need to make changes to your plan. Just answer these questions:

- What isn't working?
- What is important? (Consider the advantages and disadvantages of changing the plan.)
- What should I do about it?

Be prepared to make modifications to your solution as you go along. You will need to demonstrate skills of reflection and thinking as inevitably some mistakes will happen along the way! Keep cross-referencing aspects of planning, investigation and evaluation so that you can see what has worked well and where there is room for improvement.

TIPS

Literacy: If your design solution has a written component or comes with written instructions, ensure that you are using the correct terminology. This will also be the case during the investigation stage of the design cycle. It's important to know that you have a good grasp of your subject and can articulate your thoughts clearly and directly. Get someone to proofread what you have written, and then act on advice you are given.

EVALUATE

The key design cycle components are:

- evaluate your product/solution
- evaluate your use of the design cycle.

Throughout the design cycle process, you will have already been reviewing and evaluating your ideas, as well as modifying and refining what will hopefully be a successful end product.

The evaluation stage of the design cycle is by no means intended to happen at the end of the design cycle process but should be part of a continuous process to enable you to **review**, **modify** and **refine** your product(s). You can learn to be critical about your own work and show your ability to reflect on the process as a whole. Integral to this is also your ability to think about what you have done.

Remember that your project is going to have an audience—even if it is only one person. Something as simple as ensuring the layout of every page you submit is consistent can make your project look and feel professional. Keep the reader in mind!

TIPS

Communicating the success of your product

You may be pitching your final product for a contest, or it could just be to your teacher—either way, it's important that you communicate clearly. This takes practice! If you are presenting your work to an audience, you might like to think about the following.

- If you are using technology in your presentation, ensure it works. Have a run-through beforehand just to test things out, such as the time your presentation will take.
- If you are giving a verbal presentation, don't speak too quickly. There can be a tendency to rush through. DON'T! Savour the moment. (You can find more information on this in Chapter 5 "Presentation skills".)
- Make allowances for your audience and don't take it for granted they will understand everything you are presenting. A good communicator is both responsible and aware of their audience. Try to engage and involve wherever possible.

TIPS

Before submitting your final project:

- make sure the work is well presented and reads clearly
- don't take it for granted that the person or people assessing the work will fill in the gaps you have left out (remember that they may be looking at the work for the first time and will not be able to guess what you were thinking if the evidence isn't there)
- try your work out with a "test audience" beforehand (hopefully they will give you some good advice about what you might need to change)
- good communication will demonstrate your understanding of the task, so ensure it is clear, concise and effective.

Reflecting

The most important ATL skill you will develop in this stage of the design cycle is reflection. Becoming an excellent evaluator enables you to become a better, more reflective learner—so you can think about what might work better next time, as well as recognizing what has worked well.

Here are some tips and thoughts on the "evaluate" part of the design cycle.

Being self-aware

The evaluation process allows you to gain a better understanding of your strengths and weaknesses as a learner. While you may think that you have limitations, evaluating your work is a chance for you to see how you can overcome these limitations and maximize your potential.

Evaluation will enable you to ask yourself good questions about how you can improve and what tools you need to do so. It is also a good opportunity for you to discuss your work with both your peer group and teacher.

Analysing success

The evaluation stage of the design cycle is about analysing the success of what you have created or done and how you can further improve that creation.

SEE, THINK, WONDER ROUTINE

Choose any household object for this activity—a spoon, mobile phone, plate, etc.

What do you see? Reflect on the object's function and make notes on what you see.

What does what you see make you think? Does it give you a clue as to what makes it work so successfully?

What does the object make you wonder about what you see? Think about the design process that was involved. Write down three or four things that will help you to start thinking reflectively.

This exercise is a simple way of objectively evaluating and reflecting on any aspect of your own project. It is called a "see, think, wonder" routine:

1. What do you see?
2. What does what you see make you think?
3. What does the object make you wonder about what you see?

Using these three questions is an effective way of structuring your evaluation response.

ACTIVITY

ATL skills: reflection

Time: 15 minutes

Individual

TIPS

Try to balance the positive with the negative. Don't use this as an exercise in self-congratulation, nor in giving yourself a hard time. Balance is everything!

Telling the difference between a good and bad evaluation

Evaluation example A

My "sustainable chicken coop" project went okay. I spent a little while coming up with ideas but nothing really stood out as being particularly earth-shatteringly good so I just went through some farming websites on the internet until I came up with what I thought would be the best solution. The final design was based on an image I saw on Google Images, I thought it looked fairly straightforward to make. The end result wasn't very good as I didn't order the materials on time and Miss Jones didn't really give me much help. I didn't really stick to the design cycle as I didn't really understand it. As to whether it is sustainable, I don't really know but hope so.

Feedback

It looks as though this student hasn't really grasped the idea of evaluating. Thoughts and reflections, although honest, are rather superficial. It looks as though research has been carried out from limited sources and there is little enthusiasm for the process, leading to a rather one-dimensional evaluation. It also looks as though the student might be trying to apportion blame to his or her teacher for the project's shortcomings. Technical language is also limited and doesn't tell the writer, let alone the reader, the whole story.

Evaluation example B

My "sustainable chicken coop" project was a really good way of introducing us all to the benefits of the design cycle. It meant that we could go through the four strands of the design process (plan, investigate, create and evaluate) meticulously to help us come up with a "best fit" solution to the project brief, which was to create a design for a sustainable poultry coop using found materials. I learned a lot about my own approach to learning and how ATL helped me to underpin the various aspects of the project. During the planning stage, I found that I had a tendency to over-complicate my designs by making unnecessary additions. In retrospect, I would have limited myself both in terms of time and numbers of drawn prototypes, which would have enabled me to work with greater efficiency.

Feedback

This student has really understood the importance of evaluating. It's clear that the student is thoroughly engaged in the design process and the language used demonstrates that even though they may not be completely satisfied with their approach to learning, they have managed, through a process of critical evaluation and self-reflection to pinpoint what could be improved if they were to undertake the project again. The student writes with enthusiasm and interest. The evaluation is articulate and engaging.

Evaluation sentences

Use the following sentences in your evaluation.

I was pleased with the way my project went today because …
One of the hardest things I need to work on at the moment is …
*One of the things I could do to improve my organization effectively
is …*
I tend to work more effectively when …
My knowledge of the various tools that can help me …
*My ability to solve problems by finding creative solutions is …
because …*
Looking back through my design work regularly is important because …
The benefits of demonstrating good reflection in my work are …

> *ATL skills: reflection, organization*

MAKING REVISIONS TO THE DESIGN (OR WHAT TO DO IF THINGS DON'T GO ACCORDING TO PLAN)

The final section in this chapter will give you some examples of what students have done when their projects haven't gone according to plan. Here are some tips for you to try.

Scenario

I spent hours and hours drafting an investigation on my laptop and the power failed. I hadn't backed up any of it. Disaster! It was so frustrating but I couldn't go into class empty-handed so I bullet-pointed all the main information I was due to hand in and asked my teacher (very nicely!) for a short extension. I will never forget to back my work up again!

Scenario

I made the mistake of sharing a bit too much information with one of my friends and there was an uncanny resemblance between the two pieces of work we handed in (some bits were practically identical). The brief we were set was open-ended, so we could understand the importance of good planning. Our teacher took both of us aside and asked us to each modify some of our planning steps. I was really angry at first but, actually, I reviewed, modified and refined my plan and I got a better product out of it.

Scenario

I only had one more day to finish my evaluation but I left my project at school. The whole final project was supposed to be in for final assessment by 9 a.m. I could have tried to get into school early and to write the whole evaluation (I had about two hours' work in total to complete). But, the earliest I could have got in is 8 a.m. What saved me? I actually kept a reflective journal with notes on the project and managed to use a lot of the information I had collected throughout the project for the evaluation, which I then supplemented with the actual project the next morning!

SOME FINAL THOUGHTS ON THE DESIGN CYCLE

Used effectively, the design cycle, along with ATL, should enable you to:

- carry out your projects with efficiency and attention to detail
- understand the four crucial stages of the design process.

Although initially developed for use in technology, the design cycle—from purpose to practice—can be used effectively across all subjects.

KEY POINTS OF THE CHAPTER

ATL skills

- Organization
- Information literacy
- Communication
- Thinking
- Transfer
- Investigate
- Plan
- Create
- Evaluate

Useful websites

http://www.evernote.com

http://youtube/tUTzeEI4yUc

http://www.zerorobotics.org

Many useful design ideas can be found at:

http://designmuseum.org/

http://www.craftscouncil.org.uk/

http://www.vam.ac.uk/

http://www.dyson.co.uk/

http://www.sciencemuseum.org.uk/

http://www.vitsoe.com/en/gb/about/dieterrams/gooddesign

http://www.wired.co.uk/news/archive/2009-09/28/grand-designers-the-worlds-best-design-work

http://www.wallpaper.com/

SCIENTIFIC METHOD

Objectives for this chapter are for you to learn how to:

- create a question and research your subject
- develop an hypothesis
- test your hypothesis by running an experiment
- analyse the data you collect
- draw a conclusion about your hypothesis
- report your findings.

The scientific method is used by scientists to ensure their work is accurate, reliable and verifiable. However, it doesn't have to be used just for science—it can be useful in other subjects too. You can use this method to help solve any puzzle, unravel any mystery or carry out any investigation. The scientific method is simply the most effective way to make an inquiry or run an investigation in order to make sure you get good useful information. It starts with a prediction of what you think might happen in a certain situation and then uses an experiment to see if you were right or not. Simple!

Organization – you will need to organize your time, your materials and your process

Collaboration – you may use the scientific method by yourself, but often when you are running an experiment you will find it is easier if you work with other students

Communication – in any scientific work, it is very important to keep good records and write a clear report of everything that happened so that another person could use your work and duplicate your experiment. You will need to write it up in a way that clearly communicates your ideas to the reader

Carrying out a scientific investigation requires these skills

Information literacy – you will need to research information, analyse data, draw conclusions and create a report and process

Reflection – is often needed when things don't quite go right the first time and you need to work out what went wrong, make changes and try again

Thinking – creative thinking is needed to generate ideas for research and to design an experiment; analytical thinking is needed to analyse the results and draw conclusions

This chapter contains all the steps you need to take in order to run a scientific inquiry and so could be used as one complete exercise from idea generation to write-up. In addition, there will also be small example exercises to do at each stage.

You can use this chapter to help you design and carry out a scientific project, either by following through the whole process one step at a time from the beginning to the end, or by going straight to the step that is most relevant to your context and working from there.

CREATE A QUESTION

Every experiment starts with a question—who, what, where, when, why, how …?

Some of the greatest discoveries ever have come from asking questions. For example, "What would happen if I was in a lift in a skyscraper, falling at terminal velocity, and I took a set of keys out of my pocket and threw them up in the air?" is attributed to Einstein as the question that led him to the idea of relativity.

EXAMPLE

In 1989, Tim Berners-Lee, while working at CERN in Switzerland, was bothered by the vast quantities of information that he had to process and asked the question, "Would it be possible to transmit and access information computer to computer through some sort of file-sharing system?" and the World Wide Web was born. You might have seen him at the London 2012 Olympic opening ceremony. Search on YouTube for the clip.

For the scientific method to work, your question has to be about something that can be measured—how high, how many, how long, etc. So questions such as, "How big is the universe?" or, "How many ice creams can I eat before I explode?" would not be great questions because you couldn't really measure the answer. It is also very difficult to measure things such as anger, confusion, friendship, humour because these are very subjective things—different for every person.

ACTIVITY

ATL skills: thinking

 Time: 10 minutes

 Individual

ASKING GOOD QUESTIONS

On a piece of paper draw two columns and in one column write down some of the things you are interested in, things you enjoy doing. And then, in the other column, write down some things you don't know about each one. See if you can write in at least two things for each.

Example

Your interests	Questions
Piano	What are modern piano keys made out of?
	How many keys are there on a piano?
	How big is the biggest piano in the world?
Soccer	How many teenagers in the world play soccer?
	In which country is soccer the most popular sport?
	At what air pressure does a soccer ball burst?
The planets	If you were able to drive a car to all the planets in our solar system, how long would it take you to get to each one?
	What would you have to do to survive on each of the planets?
Shopping	Where is the biggest shopping mall in the world?
	In which country do people do the most shopping?

What can you measure?

Now it's time to start thinking about measurability.

1. Quantitative

These measurements are what we use to come up with what is called *quantitative data*— measurements of stuff that comes in quantities, for example:

- **Time:** How long does it take for …? What time of day does …?
- **Distance:** How far will …? How long is …? How tall is …?
- **Weight:** What would I weigh if I …? How much weight does a plant lose if …?
- **Volume:** How does the volume of … change when …? What is the volume of gas produced by …?
- **Temperature:** At what temperature does …? What is the melting/freezing temperature of …?
- **Number:** How many people …? How many bacteria …? How many cars …?
- **pH:** After two days the bacterial solution was at pH … whereas the yeast solution was at pH …
- **Current, voltage, amperage, power:** The solar cell produced … watts of power but the bicycle dynamo produced … watts.
- **Force:** 10kg on the end of a 1m lever produced … nm but 1kg on a 3m lever produced … nm.

2. Qualitative

These measurements are what we use to come up with what is called *quantitative data*— measurements of stuff that comes in quantities, for example:

There is also another type of scientific investigation that focuses on the gathering of *qualitative data*. This is where you are trying to get an accurate idea of what people think or feel or understand about something. Gathering qualitative data is usually done in a variety of ways, such as:

- conducting a survey of opinion
- compiling a questionnaire
- getting a large number of people to try something and then say how much they like it
- doing before and after trials.

Here are some examples of gathering qualitative data.

- Which do you like most—drink A, B, C or D?
- How well did the students do in mathematics who listened to an hour of heavy metal music compared with the students who listened to an hour of Chopin?
- What are the characteristics of the students who get the best marks at school?

Gathering qualitative data is sometimes easier than gathering quantitative data but it is also more likely to be vague and imprecise. When asking people's opinions of things or how they think or feel about a subject it is always very difficult to pin them down to a specific answer, and so analysing the data and drawing clear conclusions can be problematic. Also, as in the examples above it is always very hard to pin down a specific performance to one set of behaviours. In addition, people's performance and opinions often change depending on factors outside the experiment. Unless you are very, very keen on this kind of experimenting I would suggest you stick to coming up with a question that seeks to gather quantitative data—hard facts.

web links

 If you are doing this for a science fair project or something similar you might like to look at what other students have done at websites such as http://www.sciencebuddies.org/science-fair-projects/project_ideas.shtml. You will find lots of ideas that have been tried before that work well as a science display.

RESEARCH YOUR SUBJECT

Find out everything you can about your subject.

- Go to the library and find the right books.
- Do a web search.
- Ask someone at home.
- See if you can find anyone who is an expert in the area you are interested in and talk to them.

One good way to start searching for the right information is to make a list of key words that relate to your topic. The easiest way to do this is to look up your topic in a large dictionary or encyclopedia—there you will find lots of related key words.

So, if your topic of interest is **solar energy** your list might be:

- solar
- energy
- sun
- photovoltaic
- power
- heat
- cells.

Then ask yourself those same questions—who, what, where, when , how and why?

- Where is the best place for generating solar energy?
- What are solar cells made of?
- Why are solar cells so expensive?
- Which country makes the best solar cells?

- How do solar cells work?
- Who sells solar energy systems locally?
- When were solar cells invented?

TIPS

The aims of your research are to find out the following.

1. What is something interesting in this area that you could investigate?

2. Has anyone done an experiment similar to or the same as what you are thinking of doing?

3. What equipment/resources did they need to do it?

4. How difficult/easy was it to do the experiment?

5. What was their result?

At this point, while you are doing your research, one very important thing to make sure you do is to make a list of every source of information you find or use. Before you start looking for information, get a notebook organized and then while you are researching write down every website you find, every book you look at, every scientific paper you read and every person you talk to. Teachers are always very impressed by large reference lists—as long as all the references are relevant. Remember, it is always a complete pain when you are finally writing up your project to have to go back and find all the references you used. Just make sure for each reference you have all the relevant information:

- date you found the information
- name of author
- title of book or paper
- page number of the piece of information that was relevant to you
- publication date of the book or paper
- place of publication of the book
- full web address of useful sites including http://
- name and job title of any person who helped you.

This list eventually will become your bibliography.

It sounds like a lot of work but a bit of forethought during the research phase can save you loads of time at the write-up stage.

ACTIVITY

ATL skills: thinking, collaboration, communication

 Time: 5–15 minutes

 Group

Causality: How a change in one thing **brings about** (causes) a change in another.

ASKING SPECIFIC QUESTIONS

Write your topic area of interest at the top of a page. Underneath that heading come up with at least two questions for each of the following headings.

Who?	What?
Where?	When?
Why?	How?

DEVELOP AN HYPOTHESIS

In any experiment, what a scientist is looking for is **causality**.

It is very important to distinguish between "causality" and "correlation". "Causality" means that the cause of an event has been absolutely determined. Here are some examples.

The 1854 cholera epidemic in London was found to be caused by people drinking contaminated water from public water pumps that drew their water downstream from London, and not from those that drew their water upstream from London.

The cause of Johnny's car stopping in the middle of the road was that it had run out of petrol!

The cause of the missing sausages from on the top of the kitchen bench was found to be the cat.

"Correlation" simply means that two things occur together, as in the following example.

A direct correlation has been proven between the incidence of colour TV sets and the incidence of coronary heart disease. But does one cause the other? Although sitting watching TV may be a contributing factor to a lifestyle that increases the likelihood of developing heart disease, there is no direct **causal** link between the two. If you watch the news carefully on TV you will see a lot of correlation disguised as scientific evidence—engaging with PlayStation, Xbox, YouTube, Facebook **causes** poor performance in school. There may be a correlation between the two but you cannot say that one causes the other.

There is a direct correlation between the ownership of colour TV sets and the occurrence of heart disease in males over 40 across the world.

Does this mean that colour TV causes heart disease?

An hypothesis is simply an educated guess about a causal connection. It is a prediction of what you think might happen when you do your experiment.

When I do **this** I think **that** will happen.

Every hypothesis has two variables:

1. the **independent variable**—which is the thing that you, as the scientist, are going to change, and
2. the **dependent variable**—which is the thing that you are looking to be changed as a result.

Here is an example.

Hypothesis: The addition of small amounts of phosphate to soil increases grass growth.
Independent variable: Phosphate.
Dependent variable: Plant growth—which may be measured by difference in heights of grown grass.

In any experiment, though, there are also usually a large number of **controlled variables**. These are the things that you are trying to keep exactly the same in every part of your experiment in order to make sure any result you get can only be caused by your independent variable. In the above example the controlled variables are: soil composition, grass seed type and quantity, amount and strength of sunlight, amount of water, temperature, air flow, humidity, etc.

All these controlled variables must be kept exactly the same in each sample throughout the experiment so that any observed difference in grass growth in the samples can then be attributed to the thing you are investigating—the addition of small amounts of phosphate to one sample.

Lastly, you need to think about your **control**.

Establishing a control is the heart of every quantitative experiment. The control is simply the sample that receives no treatment, the one that receives none of the independent variable—in this case, a sample of grass seed grown in soil to which no phosphate has been added.

ACTIVITY

ATL skills: thinking, collaboration, communication

 Time: 30 minutes to 1 hour

  Group or Individual

CREATING AN HYPOTHESIS AND IDENTIFYING VARIABLES

a) Look at the list of questions you wrote for the previous exercise and see if any of them could be explored by making an hypothesis and running an experiment.
b) Write out the question you are going to try to answer with your experiment.
c) Identify your independent variable, your dependent variable and what your controlled variables will be.
d) Consider the following questions and try changing your question, your hypothesis and your proposed experiment until you satisfy the conditions listed.

What you need to do at this stage is to think about the following aspects of your experiment.

1. Is my independent variable easily measurable and able to be changed during the experiment?
2. Am I clear about what my control is?
3. Is my dependent variable easily measured?
4. Will changes in my dependent variable be due only to changes in my independent variable?
5. Are all my controlled variables identified?
6. Can all my controlled variables be well controlled so they are the same in every trial?

The key to a good experiment is **only changing one variable at a time**, keeping all other variables constant. Then, if and when you notice a measurable change in your dependent variable you can say you have noticed a causal relationship and you are then in a position to make valid predictions.

RUN AN EXPERIMENT

First, design your experiment on paper, keeping in mind all the variables mentioned in the last section. In order to give your experiment scientific validity you will probably need to run it more than once. This means that you will need to write out a very detailed experimental procedure so that you can duplicate the experiment the same way a few times in order to see if you get the same result each time.

EXPERIMENTAL CHECKLIST

Complete the following checklist.

- [ ] My topic is:
- [ ] My question is:
- [ ] My hypothesis is:
- [ ] The experiment I am going to run is:
- [ ] My independent variable will be:
- [ ] My dependent variable will be:
- [ ] My control will be:
- [ ] My controlled variables will be:
- [ ] The steps I am going to take are:

ACTIVITY

ATL skills: thinking, collaboration, communication

Time: 30 minutes to 1 hour

Group or Individual

Use of variables

If you think that changing only one variable (the amount of phosphate) in order to look for one resulting change (more grass growth) is just too simple, you could try running an experiment where you change more than one variable.

For example, if you had proved that increased phosphate led to increased grass growth in your samples that were indoors you might want to check to see if the same thing would happen to grass outdoors. In this case you will be keeping your independent and dependent variables the same and using a change in one controlled variable to give you extra data. In this example, by the end of the experiment you would know if phosphate levels caused changes in grass growth and you would also know what effect changing environments had on that causal connection.

Other controlled variables you could experiment with in this example would include the following.

- Temperature—grow the grass at two different ambient temperatures.
- Soil type—grow the grass in two soils of different composition.
- Seed varieties—use two different varieties of seed in each part of the experiment.

Just make sure that for each part of the experiment you have at least two samples—one that receives the independent variable (the phosphate) and one that doesn't. The one that receives no phosphate is then the **control** against which any extra growth will be compared.

If you maintain the same conditions for the control and the experimental sample in every environment and only vary the phosphate levels in the experimental sample, then your experiment will yield valid data. If you do it this way you are also putting more variety into your data. When you write up the experiment you will not only be able to conclude whether your added phosphate level increased grass growth or not, but you will also be able to talk about the different effects in different environments, which will make the data much more interesting.

Of course, if you want some really comprehensive data you could also run trials in each environment with different levels of phosphate. You will still need a control in each environment (a sample that receives no phosphate) but you could have four other samples in each environment, each with a different level of phosphate:

- one with 0.01g of added phosphate per kg of soil
- one with 0.1g/kg
- one with 1g/kg
- one with 10g/kg.

Then you will be able to see if increasing phosphate increases grass growth continuously or if there is a cut-off point above which it doesn't help. If it worked like that, then what you would have is not just causality but a causal relationship that lends itself to being graphed and will provide endless material for discussion. Teachers love stuff like that!

GRAPHING EXPERIMENTAL DATA

Draw a line graph of % phosphate against grass growth using the information below.

Once you have drawn it, comment on its shape. What does that tell you about phosphate in soil and grass growth?

Are there any other types of graph you could use to represent this data? What are they called?

Amount of phosphate added to the soil in g/kg soil	Grass growth in weight of dry matter over a 5-day period
0.00	30
0.01	31
0.05	33
0.10	36
0.50	54
1.00	68
5.00	38

Sample size

The last thing to think about when you run an experiment is **sample size**. If you do just one experiment with one sample and one control, then it may be very hard to draw good conclusions about causality because the result might have happened by chance. To increase the validity of your conclusion:

- repeat the experiment several times in exactly the same way

or

- have a larger number of samples or trials in your experiment.

As a rule of thumb, the recommended number is:

- 5 samples or 5 repeats at the middle school or MYP level
- 10 samples or 10 repeats at the high school or Diploma Programme level, and
- 20 samples or 20 repeats at the university level.

To be sure about this, it is probably best to ask your teacher when you are at the experimental design stage.

Once you have decided on all your experimental variables you will need to write out every step in the experiment as a procedure to follow each time the experiment is run. The easiest way to do this is to run through the experiment in a pretend way with all the right equipment and write down or get an observer to write down everything that you do—every single step. It is important to detail everything that happens because the key to running good experiments is being able to duplicate the experiment exactly, every time, changing only the thing you want to change.

When you come to run the experiment properly, if you change anything at all make sure you write down exactly what you changed.

ACTIVITY

ATL skills: thinking, collaboration, communication

 Time: 30 minutes

  Group or Individual

WRITING THE EXPERIMENTAL PROCEDURE

Write out your experimental procedure. Your aim is to have a written procedure that anyone could follow and duplicate exactly what you did—even if they knew nothing at all about the experiment.

web links

 Here are some good websites with graphic organizers that you can use to help you write up your whole experimental procedures.

Search online for 'barnett.nebo.edu' and 'scientific method' for an excellent worksheet.

http://contentbuilder.merlot.org/toolkit/uploads/49241/scientific_method_graphic_organizer.jpg

ANALYSE THE DATA YOU COLLECT

After looking at the data you collected from your experiment, ask yourself if you have enough to draw some conclusions about your hypothesis. If not, repeat the experiment until you do.

What you are looking for with all your data is some kind of relationship or lack of relationship between your variables. In other words, a way in which changes in your independent variable affected your dependent variable. There are different relationships you might be able to comment on.

Direct relationship

- More (or less) of A always produces more (or less) of B, as in these examples.
  - The more CO_2 there is in the atmosphere the warmer the air temperature will be.
  - The more sugar there is in a drink the sweeter it will taste.
  - The more you pay attention in class the more you will learn.

Indirect relationship

- More (or less) of A sometimes produces more (or less) of B depending on C, as in these examples.
  - More rewards for good behaviour sometimes produces better behaved children, depending on the nature of individual children.
  - More punishments for bad behaviour sometimes produces better behaved children, depending on the nature of individual children.
  - More sunshine produces more plant growth, depending on the type of plant.
- More (or less) of A produces more (or less) of B up to a point where there is just too much A, and B stops changing, as in these examples.
  - More fertilizer produces more plant growth up to the point where the fertilizer becomes poisonous.
  - More food produces less hunger up the point where you feel full.

There may be no discernable relationship at all, in which case you can then say that changes in A do not affect B at all.

Although there are many ways to analyse data, the simplest way is probably to create a table—for example, of grass growth height against amount of phosphate—and then from the table draw a graph.

TIPS

Always remember, the word data is **plural**!

In other words, you should say:

- *the data are,* **not** *the data is*
- *the data show,* **not** *the data shows*
- *the data relate to,* **not** *the data relates to*

Scientists will notice if you get this wrong, so it is best to get it right!

Usually when we draw a graph of experimental data we put the independent variable on the X-axis (horizontal) and the dependent variable on the Y-axis (vertical). You might choose a bar graph or a time-series plot, or an XY-line graph, or a pie chart, or one of many others. The type of graph you choose will depend on the type of data you have and the point you want to prove. If you enter your data into Excel it will give you many options as to how you can present them as a graph. Make sure you label both your axes correctly and that all your units are correct.

If you end up with an XY-line graph and you get a good consistent line you may be able to describe it mathematically. If it is a straight line, then it is relatively easy to work out the formula for the line. To do this you need to consider 3 things: the slope, the direction of the line and where the line cuts the Y-axis.

XY-line graph

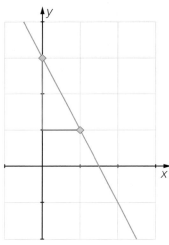

1. Look at the slope. Slope = rise/run, that is the number of units on the Y-axis over the number of units on the X-axis. For example, if your line goes up 2 on the Y-axis and out 1 on the X-axis, then you can say that the slope is 2/1 = 2.
2. Look at the direction of the line. If the slope of your line is going down from left to right it is a negative slope and if it is going up from left to right it is a positive slope. In the example on the left it is a negative slope (–2).
3. Look at where the line cuts the Y-axis, In the example, the line cuts the Y-axis at positive 1.5.

Now you can put all those bits together and you get the formula for the line, which is:

$$y = -2x + 1.5$$

Which by rearrangement will also tell you that:

$$x = -0.5y + 0.75$$

Which you could then use to predict further values of y and x outside your experimental parameters. All of which may or may not be useful to you.

If the line you create is a curved line, then the mathematics is more complicated but can still be done.

One thing you are always looking for in your data is **significance**.

If something is significant it means that it didn't happen by chance.

CASE STUDY

Food poisoning

Three people who ate together at a local restaurant all have food poisoning.

It is your job to find out if this is significant. Does it mean that they got the food poisoning from the restaurant, or did they get it from somewhere else?

Before you could begin to work out if the problem was at the restaurant you would have to know:

- how many people eat in the restaurant every day
- how often food poisoning normally occurs in this community.

If you found out that:

- a total of 500 people a day eat at the restaurant
- on any average day 6 people in 1,000 gets food poisoning in your city.

Then you would probably say that this case is not significant. However, what if 10 people who ate there got food poisoning? Or 20 people, or 50 people? At some point you would probably start to think that such an occurrence couldn't have happened by chance and you would start to think that the restaurant must be to blame. This is where you have determined that the result is significant.

Significance is usually worked out by statistical methods. This type of analysis of results usually happens in the "Discussion" section of your scientific report.

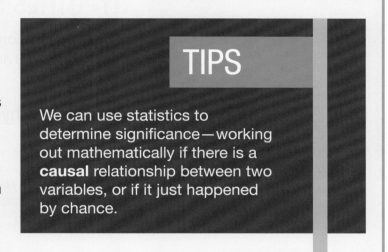

TIPS

We can use statistics to determine significance—working out mathematically if there is a **causal** relationship between two variables, or if it just happened by chance.

In statistics we have what is called a **significance level** that we can work out to see how significant any relationship is. If we can say through our statistical analysis of the data that a relationship is significant at the 5% level, then what we are saying is that 5% of the time we could have got that same result purely by chance, so that 95% of the time that particular result must be due to the change that we made in our experiment. Scientists are very precise, though, and usually won't settle for significance at the 5% level. Usually something has to be significant at the 1% level (only 1 time in 100 that result could have happened by chance) or preferably at the 0.1% level (only 1 time in 1,000 could that result have happened by chance) before they are happy to say a relationship is significant. If you want to know more about this type of analysis ask your mathematics or statistics teacher.

DRAW A CONCLUSION ABOUT YOUR HYPOTHESIS

In your conclusion you are referring back to your hypothesis and deciding if the evidence is strong enough to confirm or deny your hypothesis.

Restate your hypothesis

Example

Based on my research and my own experience I predicted that when I increased the phosphate levels in the soil I would grow more grass.

Summarize the results of your experiment

Example

What actually happened was that I got more grass growth in my samples, compared to my control, for each increase in phosphate from 0.01g/kg soil up to 1g/kg, above which I got a drop in grass growth.

TIPS

Be very clear and stick only to the facts—no opinions, no guesses, no thoughts of what should have happened, none of your ideas—just the facts. Remember to describe any observed or calculated relationship (or lack of the same) between your independent and dependent variables. It isn't a failure if you didn't prove your hypothesis true—that is also interesting and useful information.

Include key findings from your research

These will back up and support the results that you did get.

Example

Grass needs phosphate for growth. One of the key fertilizers used by farmers to boost grass growth to feed cows is called "super-phosphate" and is a soluble form of phosphate very similar to what was used in this example.

Increased levels of phosphate can boost growth of grass up to a point where the phosphate becomes poisonous to the plant. Several cases have been reported of farmers accidently putting too much "super-phosphate" on a particular paddock and actually killing off all the grass.

State whether your results support or contradict your hypothesis

Be careful about being sure.

- How certain are you about the predictability of the relationship you have demonstrated through your experiment?
- Will it be a true relationship in every situation?
- Can you think of any situations in which the result you obtained might not happen?

In drawing your conclusion make sure you stick to exactly what you proved in your experiment, nothing more. Remember a negative finding, one that does not support your hypothesis, can be just as valuable as a positive finding. If that is the case, think about what that means. What conclusions can you draw based on your finding that your hypothesis was not correct? Does that mean that an alternative hypothesis might be correct? If so, state that hypothesis as a possibility—an area for further study.

Make some comments on your experimental method. Did your experiment go the way you planned it would, or not? If you had the chance to do it all again what changes would you make to the process?

Do your results suggest to you a direction for further study? Can you think of any further experiments that could be performed to take your results further or to confirm your results from another direction?

REPORT YOUR FINDINGS

Write up the whole process, including everything mentioned so far.

Your final report will probably need to include all the following,
usually in this order.

Summary	Also known as an abstract, this is a paragraph that comes first in a scientific report and gives the reader a short summary of what you did and what you proved.

> **TIPS**
>
> It is usually best to leave the writing of the summary until last—even though it comes first in your report.

Table of contents	If your report is quite long you will need to include this to enable people to find what they want.
Topic and research	This sets out what your topic is, why you are interested in it, what you discovered in your research, which area you ended up deciding to investigate and what attracted you to it.
Research question	What was the question you were trying to answer?
Hypothesis	What was the causal relationship you wanted to explore?
Experimental design	Why did you choose that particular experiment?
	What was your experimental design—the idea, the equipment you needed, the general procedure you were going to use?
	What were your independent, dependent and controlled variables? What was your control?
Experimental procedure	Using a flow chart or step-by-step listing, describe all the steps you took in running each experiment, making sure you detail any changes you made in any repeat procedures.
Results	All your observations from your experiment—what actually happened—and all the data you obtained.
Analysis and discussion	What you did with your data to make sense of it and help you to draw conclusions—tables, graphs, statistical analysis.

Conclusions	Did your experimental results confirm or contradict your original hypothesis?
Comments	Any changes you would make if you did it all again, and any future directions for this line of research that have been suggested by your results.
Bibliography	All your references—books, papers, journals, websites, people who helped you.

Lastly, remember to do a spell check and get someone else to proofread it for errors and readability!

KEY POINTS OF THE CHAPTER

ATL skills

- Organization
- Collaboration
- Information literacy
- Thinking
- Reflection
- Communication

The key stages in the scientific method

1. Find a field of interest and research your subject
2. Create a question to be answered
3. Develop an hypothesis
4. Test your hypothesis by running an experiment
5. Collect data
6. Analyse the data you collect
7. Draw a conclusion about your hypothesis
8. Report your findings

Useful websites

http://barnett.nebo.edu/sites/barnett.nebo.edu/files/Scientific%20 Method%20Graphic%20Organizer.pdf

http://www.brainpop.com/science/scientificinquiry/scientificmethod/ preview.weml

http://contentbuilder.merlot.org/toolkit/uploads/49241/scientific_ method_graphic_organizer.jpg

http://www.sciencebuddies.org/science-fair-projects/project_ideas. shtml

http://www.sciencebuddies.org/science-fair-projects/project_ scientific_method.shtml

http://science.pppst.com/scientificmethod.html

http://www.sciencebob.com/sciencefair/scientificmethod.php

http://steedsstars.blogspot.com/2009/06/scientific-method-cartoon. html

PRESENTATION SKILLS

OBJECTIVES

In this chapter you will learn:

- which ATL skills will support you in creating and delivering presentations
- the key stages in producing group and individual presentations
- the key skills involved in producing different types of presentations (analytical, informative, persuasive).

Presentations can be very scary. For some students, standing up in front of a group of people can send them into a cold sweat! However, with a clear **purpose**, an **organized approach**, and **practice** it is possible to learn to overcome your fears and produce effective and engaging presentations.

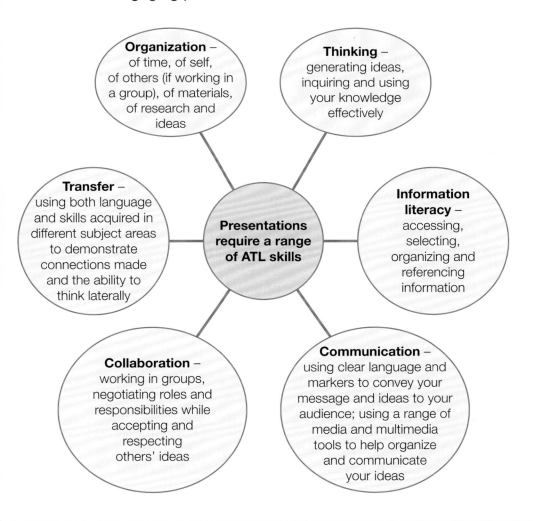

Organization – of time, of self, of others (if working in a group), of materials, of research and ideas

Thinking – generating ideas, inquiring and using your knowledge effectively

Transfer – using both language and skills acquired in different subject areas to demonstrate connections made and the ability to think laterally

Presentations require a range of ATL skills

Information literacy – accessing, selecting, organizing and referencing information

Collaboration – working in groups, negotiating roles and responsibilities while accepting and respecting others' ideas

Communication – using clear language and markers to convey your message and ideas to your audience; using a range of media and multimedia tools to help organize and communicate your ideas

In the chapter on essay-writing you read about the importance of good time management and strong research skills. These also apply to presentations. However, in this chapter we will focus on four ATL skills that are essential to your success in producing effective presentations: **thinking**, **communication**, **organization** and (for group presentations) **collaboration**.

TYPES OF PRESENTATION

During your school career, in addition to group discussions, you may be called on to perform a variety of different types of presentations, individually or in groups.

Individual

These could include the following.

- A persuasive speech on a controversial issue
- An analytical or explanatory talk on a book or film, giving your own opinion about it
- A proposal outlining improvements to an aspect of school life
- Delivering a monologue to the class in role as a character
- An informative talk on an issue or topic explaining how or why something happens

Pair/group

These could include the following.

- Group presentation on a poem you have studied in class
- Debate on school uniform where students take opposing sides on the issue
- Performing an additional scene with a partner in role as two characters in a novel
- In a pair interviewing a fellow student about their views on a local issue

Whether you are presenting alone, as a pair or in a group there are **key skills** that apply to all presentations.

- Ensuring you are clear about the ideas and information you want to share with your audience
- Making sure the information and ideas are relevant and suited to your audience

- Maintaining the interest of your audience
- Sounding confident, interested and enthusiastic about your ideas and information
- Communicating those ideas and information in a clear and concise manner using a clear structure
- Using language appropriate to your task, your purpose and your audience

THE "FOUR Ps"

The "Four Ps" of producing a presentation are illustrated in the diagram below.

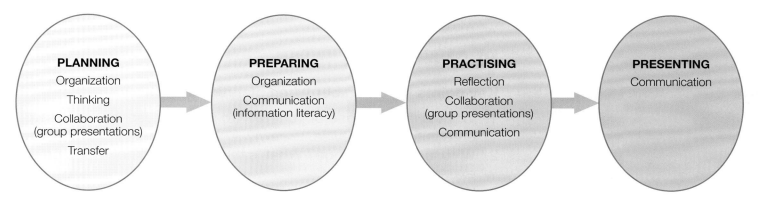

PLANNING
Organization
Thinking
Collaboration
(group presentations)
Transfer

PREPARING
Organization
Communication
(information literacy)

PRACTISING
Reflection
Collaboration
(group presentations)
Communication

PRESENTING
Communication

The "four Ps" build on four ATL skills that you are already familiar with. Let's take a look at these four skills in more detail now.

Thinking

- Generating ideas—including the use of brainstorming.
- Planning—outlining a plan.
- Inquiring—including questioning and challenging information and arguments, developing questions, using the inquiry cycle.
- Applying knowledge and concepts—including logical progression of arguments.
- Identifying problems—including deductive reasoning, evaluating solutions to problems.

Communication

- Being informed—using a variety of media.
- Literacy—using and interpreting a range of content-specific terminology.
- Informing others—including presentation skills using a variety of media.

Organization

- Time management—including using time effectively in class, keeping to deadlines.
- Self-management—including personal goal-setting, organization of learning materials.

Transfer

- Planning a presentation—which is very similar to planning an essay, so many of the techniques in Chapter 2 "The writing process" are relevant here.
- Making connections—including using knowledge, understanding and skills across subjects to create products or solutions.

PLANNING YOUR PRESENTATION

ATL skills: thinking

Key points to remember when planning

1. What is the **purpose** of your talk (to inform, describe, analyse, entertain, argue, revise, review)?
2. **Who** is your **audience**? What is their previous knowledge or experience?
3. **What** do you want them to learn? What **main points** do you want to make?
4. What is the **context**? Formal or informal situation?
5. **How** are you going to get that information across most effectively?

TIPS

To help you remember these elements in your planning, think about PATCH.

- **P**urpose—what are you trying to achieve? What is your aim?
- **A**udience—who are you talking to?
- **T**opic—what is the presentation about? What are the main ideas?
- **C**ontext—where is the venue, what is the situation?
- **H**ow can you communicate your message most effectively?

Thinking about PURPOSE

Thinking about the purpose is crucial to your presentation. Are you trying to persuade or convince people about something, entertain them, or inform them about an issue or topic? The purpose will affect the **type of language** you use, the **style of your delivery** and **the information** you decide to include.

Argue: Challenge or debate an issue or idea with the purpose of persuading or committing someone else to a particular stance or action.

Discuss: Offer a considered and balanced review that includes a range of arguments, factors or hypotheses. Opinions or conclusions should be presented clearly and supported by appropriate evidence.

Persuade: Present a case for or against an issue, trying to convince someone of your opinion using supporting evidence.

PURPOSE

Explain: Give a detailed account including reasons or causes.

Describe: Give a detailed account or picture of a situation, event, pattern or process.

Inform: Provide interesting, useful and objective factual information.

Analyse: Break down in order to bring out the essential elements or structure, to identify parts and relationships, and to interpret information to reach conclusions.

Very often your presentation may involve more than one of these purposes. For example, a discussion on a current issue may require you to:

- **explain** the key issues and arguments
- **analyse** the main arguments, and
- **persuade** people to agree with your point of view.

The purpose will determine the structure, language and style of your presentation. You will need to adapt your language and your content to suit your audience and think about how you can best organize and present your material so that it is engaging and informative.

Thinking about AUDIENCE

It is important to think about your audience as you will need to adapt your material and language to ensure they understand you and to engage their interest in order to communicate your message. Often you will be addressing your classmates—who you should know well—but sometimes you will need to present to an examiner (a teacher) or deliver a talk to an unfamiliar audience.

When considering your audience you could think about some of the following factors.

- What do they already know about your topic?
- What do they want to know about your topic?
- How do they feel about an issue?
- What are their expectations from your talk?
- What are their cultural and educational backgrounds?
- What is their ability in your subject or topic area?
- What are their prejudices and biases?
- Are there any second-language speakers?
- What is their mood likely to be?

Think about your audience as learners and how you can keep them engaged. In Chapter 1 "Learning about learning" you were introduced to different sensory preferences for learning and you should consider how they relate to your audience and how you can reach them in your presentation. Ask yourself:

- Are they visual learners (respond well to images)?
- Are they auditory learners (respond well to talk)?
- Are they kinesthetic learners (need to do something and be actively involved)?

The answer is they are probably a mixture of all these learning styles, so you need to try to cater to them all as learners. Think about what strategies will help you do this.

APPEALING TO YOUR AUDIENCE

What could you include in your presentation to address the different sensory learning preferences of your audience? Below are some suggested tools and ideas. Using these and your own ideas, complete the table below.

Images, music, question-and-answer session

Slides, internet links, handouts

Activities, props, questionnaire, survey

Learning style	Learning aids
Visual	
Auditory	
Kinesthetic	

ACTIVITY

ATL skills: thinking, communication

Time: 5 minutes

Individual

TIPS

Since listening to someone talk at you is sometimes very difficult, try to think about your audience as being made up of people with different learning styles. Visual and other non-verbal tools can be very helpful.

Thinking about TOPIC

Become an expert in your subject

The content of your presentation is crucial. One of the keys to help you overcome a fear of presenting is to know your topic very well. Many people are afraid that they will run out of things to say. A detailed knowledge of WHAT you are talking about will give you confidence.

Prior knowledge and gaps

A good starting point is to think about what your audience might already know about the topic. This will also help you think about the gaps in your own knowledge. What do you want to learn and what do you want your audience to learn about the topic? Decide on the key points you want to communicate.

Check the requirements of the task

Check the requirements of the task and be sure you are familiar with the marking criteria and are fulfilling the demands of the examiners.

Research from a range of sources

The key to becoming an expert in your topic is to explore a range of different sources on the topic (such as internet, interviews, books, magazines, personal experience/memories, films, newspapers, encyclopedias, television).

Be sure to check your facts against a reliable source and reference your materials as you go. See Chapter 2 "The writing process" about the importance of referencing your material. Record all sources and list them at the end of your presentation on a slide or handout.

Selecting your material

A common error with presentations is trying to cover too much material. Keep it short and simple—do not attempt too much. Your audience will probably only retain a fraction of the information or arguments so be sure not to overload them with facts or opinions. Obviously the content of your presentation will depend to a certain extent on the specific task and purpose of your presentation—whether it be to inform, persuade or entertain.

As a general guide try to make your talk CRISP.

Convincing—sound like you know what you are talking about.

Relevant—be sure your material is current.

Interesting—try and tell your audience something they do not know. Leave them thinking and inspired.

Supported—use evidence/statistics/opinions to add weight to your points.

Powerful—the key is to ensure you make an impact on your audience.

Thinking about CONTEXT

This is the situation, or the circumstances, in which you will be presenting. Here are the key questions to consider.

- What is the occasion— formal or informal?
- How many people am I addressing?
- How much time do I have?
- Are other people presenting on similar topics?
- What technology is available?
- How much space is there in the venue?
- How will I organize my space?
- How much time do I have to present?

AUDIENCE

+

PURPOSE

↓

LANGUAGE

Thinking about HOW to communicate your message

So far we have focused on the CONTENT of the presentation and WHAT you say. Now we need to focus on HOW you deliver your material and communicate your message, which is just as important. If your delivery style is uninteresting you will lose the interest and attention of your listeners.

When thinking about how best to communicate your ideas to your audience you should focus on the STRUCTURE and the LANGUAGE you will use.

- The **structure**:
  - the order in which you will make your points
  - how you incorporate non-verbal elements
  - how you use your introduction, topic sentences and conclusion to make an impact.

- The **language**:
  - the formality of your language
  - the language devices you use to guide your reader through your presentation
  - the different types of language you will use to suit your purpose.

STRUCTURING YOUR PRESENTATION

Prioritizing your ideas

In order to ensure you do not overload your audience with information and lose their interest it is important that you consider carefully what the most important points are and where you should make them in your speech—to maximize their impact.

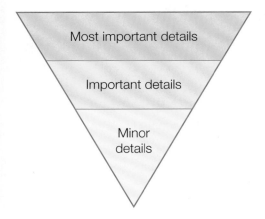

Most important details

Important details

Minor details

An inverted pyramid structure is an effective tool to help you focus on the key ideas. Newspaper reporters use it when they are writing to a word limit. Imagine someone is cutting your presentation down bit by bit. Which information would you not want to lose? This should be placed higher up the inverted pyramid.

Finding the right shape

Once you have decided on the material, you need to think about how you can best arrange it to communicate your ideas in as clear, concise and engaging a way as possible. The structure of your talk will vary according to the purpose and type of task you are asked to perform. However, there are some general points that should help you.

In terms of overall structure each presentation will differ slightly, depending on its purpose and audience, but the basic format should be:

1. tell your audience what you are going to say,
2. tell them,
3. then tell them what you have said.

Limit the number of points you try to make to around 3–5.

TIPS

You should be able to summarize the main idea of your talk in a phrase or sentence. All points should support it. Use this phrase or sentence at the beginning and end of your presentation.

web links

Check out this Ted talk "The secret structure of great talks" on the website http://www.ted.com/talks/nancy_duarte_the_secret_structure_of_great_talks.html. It is by Nancy Duarte who outlines, among other things, the power of story in communicating a message and finding the key shape to a good presentation: moving between the reality, or "what is", and the possible better alternative, "what could be".

Below are some general templates for **writing** different types of texts. Using the advice from Nancy Duarte and considering the advice that follows, think about how you would adapt them for a talk or presentation in order to add impact.

Discussions

Introduction
- Clear opening statement about the topic
- Explanation of opposing viewpoints, highlighting key issues/differences
- Anecdote

Main body
- Arguments for and against
- clear topic sentences
- supporting evidence (facts, statistics, experiences and opinions of experts/self) for each point
- analysis/explanation of that evidence
- strong closing sentence

Conclusion
- Summary highlighting key arguments
- Clear (re)statement of personal position
- Recommendation for action

Arguments

Introduction
- Clear opening statement/thesis
- Challenge to an idea
- Explanation of key issue(s)
- Key background information

Main body
- Arguments outlining your viewpoint and undermining opposing viewpoints
- clear topic sentences stating your idea(s)
- supporting evidence (facts, statistics, experiences and opinions of experts/self) to support your arguments
- strong closing sentence

Conclusion
- Summary of key points
- Clear (re)statement of position
- Recommendation for action

Analyses

Introduction
- Placing of text/extract in its wider context
- Outline of key author's main intentions and techniques
- Explanation of key effects of the intentions and techniques
- Outline of key thesis/argument

Main body
- Clear topic sentences outlining intention and technique
- Evidence from text (quotations/references)
- Opinions of critics or own personal interpretations
- Explanations and analysis of linguistic and stylistic features

Conclusion
- Summary of key ideas/techniques and effects
- Clear (re)statement of thesis
- Personal opinion

Informative

Introduction
- General statement introducing the topic
- Basic information about topic (who, what, when, where)
- Overview of key areas to be addressed

Main body
- Logical development of ideas
- Description/facts about various aspects of the subject organized by paragraph

Conclusion
- Possible concluding general statement

To help you think about how you can adapt these generic structures to suit your audience and purpose, let's explore in a little more detail the key elements of presentations.

Clear openings grab your audience's interest

The key to a good opening is to capture the audience's attention and make clear the intention and purpose of your talk. You also need to look and sound confident and clear about what your message is. Your opening might include:

- a clear statement about the topic and the areas you will address
- an anecdote to engage your audience's interest and lead them into your topic
- a fact to grab the audience's attention and make them think
- an image that you display and refer to, or ask your audience to consider
- a question to involve your audience or get them thinking about your topic.

Other things you could do in your introduction include:

- challenging your audience' s assumptions about a topic or issue
- appealing to the audience's imagination
- using rhetorical questions to engage their interest and start them thinking.

ACTIVITY

ATL skills: communication and thinking

 Time: 10 minutes

 Pairs

BEGINNING WITH A BANG

Read the following openings and note down key features of content and language. Decide what the purpose of each presentation is and see if you can note the key information or arguments being put forward. Feed back to a partner and see if you both agree on the same points.

Example A

I would like to start by asking how many of you would ever consider selling your kidney to someone in need of a transplant? It may sound gruesome but if you were desperate for money to feed your children, it is something you may consider. After all, a kidney can sell for a considerable sum of money. The key issue here is should we be allowed to choose what we do with our bodies? Many people think we should. But there are others who argue that creating a black market in body parts is both unsafe and would prey on those who are most vulnerable and desperate in society.

Example B

Good afternoon, everyone. As a group we will be analysing an extract from chapter 11 of William Golding's Lord of the Flies and commenting on Golding's portrayal of the struggle between the two opposing forces on the island and how the author uses aspects of setting, dialogue and animalistic imagery to build tension and reinforce the boys' descent into savagery. I will begin talking about the aspects of setting, then Diego will look at dialogue and Ki-Won will finish by exploring the imagery.

Example C

Frida Kahlo's work can be summarized by three Ps: Passion, Pain, Personal. I am going to help you share and experience all three by discussing both her life and the influences on her as an artist. I will focus on three key paintings: "The Two Fridas", "The Broken Column" and "A Few Small Nips". In each of these pieces I will highlight how she portrays, through both content and form, the intense pain and grief she suffered throughout her life and her tempestuous marriage to fellow Mexican muralist Diego Rivera.

Example D

I'd like you all to consider this slide and imagine yourself as one of those little six-month-old dogs crammed into a cage with thirty others. Your back has been crushed, your hair shaved and electrodes implanted in your head and tail. Blinded, all you can hear are the excruciating squeals of pain from other dogs submitted to testing bone and joint research. Next to you imprisoned rabbits bleed, blinded by the mascara forced on them. Grim. Cruel. Inhumane. Call it what you wish, but the fact is this is the stark and cruel reality of animal testing. And its purpose? To ensure mascara will not affect the human skin. Surely such inhumane torture must halt immediately.

Using transitions and discourse markers

Whether writing or speaking it is always helpful to signal to the reader or listener the different stages of your argument or discussion. The language we use to do this includes what are often referred to as "connectives", "transitions" or "discourse markers". Below is a list of some of the main ones. See if you can add to the list.

Adding information	In addition, furthermore, moreover, a further argument, additionally …
Offering contrasting opinions	In contrast, rather, on the other hand, however, alternatively, nevertheless …
Signalling different stages	Firstly, to begin, secondly, finally, in conclusion, lastly …
Giving examples	For example, for instance, as an example …
Offering similar opinions	Similarly, likewise …
Show a cause or consequence	As a result, for this reason, consequently …
Making comparisons	Whereas x … y … Unlike x, y … Like x, y also… Both x and y …

One way to signal a change in your conversation is to put these words at the beginning of a sentence or paragraph. Sometimes it is a good idea to vary their position and place them near but not at the very start of a sentence. This avoids your speech or writing sounding too repetitive.

Example

There are, however, other people who believe that …

Here, in order to emphasize the word "however", we have separated it with commas.

Building on the presentations outlined above, here are some possible transition sentences.

Another key reason why dogs should be banned from cities is …

In addition to powerful descriptions of the setting, the author also uses vivid animalistic images to convey the boys' savagery.

A further influence on Frida Kahlo was her …

Powerful endings

It is important to end your talk in an assertive and confident manner. Here are some key things to think about when writing a conclusion.

- End with a clear concluding statement that makes an impact and relates to your opening statement.
- Make your view clear on the issue if you are arguing or persuading someone.
- Relate the issue to a real-life context that your audience can relate to. This will help them connect with your ideas.
- Make it personal. Relate the issue to your own life/experiences or those of your audience.
- Leave your audience thinking.
- Quote someone famous who makes a relevant statement on your topic.
- Project your audience into the future and make them look ahead at possible scenarios (positive or negative) as a means of supporting your ideas and/or urge them to take action.

Example

To conclude, while banning dogs from cities would reduce noise pollution and provide a more hygienic environment, such a law would not only deprive millions of people of companionship, a sense of security and opportunities to get out, exercise and meet people but would also disadvantage those with physical disorders from leading a full life. For this reason we believe such a proposition is both short-sighted and unethical. Let every dog have his day in every town and city!

Incorporating evidence with illustrations and examples

Your talk is really as convincing as the evidence you offer to support your ideas. Supporting your ideas with examples and illustrations brings your points alive and personalizes your talk. Decide on the **best evidence** to support your ideas. A word of warning though—be wary of examples and verbal illustrations that can divert you from the main focus of your presentation.

Good examples can be very persuasive in making your audience sympathize with your point of view. Consider the advice and examples below.

- **Painting a vivid picture for your audience**
  Your back has been crushed, your hair shaved and electrodes implanted in your head and tail.
- **Using statistics**
  According to the National Commission for ...
  A recent report/survey/poll issued by ... states that ...
- **Including opinions**
  If you ask people on the street why they won't buy music from music stores, they will likely say, "CDs are too expensive."
  A valid point considering the rise in CD prices.
- **Using anecdotes**
  Use anecdotes from your own experience and the wider world. Often a listener will remember the anecdote and then the point that it illustrated.
- **Using humour**
  A touch of humour can make even the most uninteresting topic sound appealing. However, humour does not always mean joke-telling. A funny anecdote that supports a point can be very effective in helping your audience remember it. Sometimes a joke can help lift the mood of the room, ease any tension, and re-engage an audience.

The language of your presentation

The formality of your language

This will depend on the context of your presentation, on the audience and on the situation. Firstly you need to be aware of the differences between formal and informal speech.

TIPS

Note: If you use statistics be sure you cite the source.

ATL skill: communication

Differences between formal and informal speech

Informal	Formal
• Verbal fillers *um, ya know, I mean, like, I guess,*	• Rhetorical questions *Is this how you would treat your own car?*
• Restarts *It's like … Well, I mean it's similar to …*	• Emotive language *a crippling blow, a shocking revelation, a devastating decision, a desperate measure*
• Interruptions/overlaps *A: We tried to record our findings but it was …* *B: Yeah, that was impossible with all the noise*	• Technical language *This is a clear example of deforestation*
• Contractions *can't, didn't, couldn't, wasn't, would've*	• Use of literary devices – similes, metaphor
• Slang/colloquial language *kinda, kids, wanna, dude, chill out, check it out*	• Repetition for effect *This will produce benefits for ourselves, our children and our children's children.*
• Unplanned pauses/hesitations *Well, it was … er … around 3pm I guess*	• Discourse markers *On the other hand, furthermore, similarly*
• Incomplete sentences	• Planned pauses for dramatic effect
	• Complete sentences

Sometimes you may want your presentation to sound more personal in order to create a sense of your own belief in what you are saying. However, at other times, you may want to give your voice an air of authority to add weight to what you are saying. This requires more formal, impersonal language which is closer to the language of writing than of everyday speech. It has a planned quality about it.

How to make your speech sound more formal and impersonal

In order to make your presentation sound more formal, one thing you can do is make your language more **impersonal**. Two ways you can do this are by using:

- **nominalization**—using more nouns and fewer verbs in your speech and writing
- **passivization**—using the passive voice to make your speech or writing more polite and impersonal.

Nominalization

Formal speech or writing frequently uses *nominalizations*—that is, the noun forms of verbs and other parts of speech. When we use a verb we generally have to say who is involved in the action. Leaving out the verb allows us to hide who or what is responsible. The process of nominalization turns verbs (actions or events) into nouns (things, concepts or people). Nominalized texts focus on objects or concepts instead of actions and people. This can be very useful, particularly in persuasive or argumentative presentations.

TIPS

Do not worry if these terms seem complicated. They are merely names for things you may already be doing in your speech and writing. You may even be able to use them to impress your teacher in your own written or oral presentations!

TIGHTENING UP YOUR TALK

To help you understand how nominalization works, complete the following exercises.

In the right-hand column, underline the noun form of the verb that is italicized in the left-hand column.

Verb form	Nominalized form—more formal/impersonal
People *argue* that …	A common <u>argument</u> is …
Many people *claim* that …	The common claim that …
Everyone *agrees* that …	There is general agreement that …
Opponents *decided* that …	The decision by opponents to …
People often *assume* that …	A common assumption is that …

In the right-hand column, complete the noun form of the verb underlined in the left-hand column.

Verb form	Nominalized form—more formal/impersonal
They <u>completed</u> the project …	The _____ of the project …
Most people <u>complain</u> that …	A common _____ is that …
People have <u>suggested</u> …	The _____ to …
If you <u>observe</u> closely you will see …	Close _____ reveals …
Many people <u>use</u> plastics …	The common _____ of plastics …

Using the passive voice

Another way to make a text sound more impersonal, polite and persuasive is using the passive voice.

In the **active voice** we emphasize the **doer** or **agent** of the action.

> **Example**
>
> *Federico broke the window. (Federico is the person doing the breaking.)*

In the **passive voice** we emphasize the **done to** or **recipient** of the action.

> **Example**
>
> *The window was broken by Federico. (The window is being acted on by Federico.)*

However, we can go further using the passive and **hide the doer or agent of the action completely.**

> **Example**
>
> *The window was broken. (Here there is no mention of Federico.)*

Using impersonal language can be very useful when constructing arguments to add weight to ideas. By hiding the agent of an action or a belief you can focus on the action or belief itself without drawing attention to who performs or believes it. Returning to the statements we looked at earlier in the exercise on nominalization, we can see how converting the verbs into a passive form achieves this.

These examples also highlight another important technique to sounding impersonal and formal—and that is the use of generalized voices.

Verb form	Passive form (more impersonal)
People argue that …	It is argued that …
Many people claim that …	It is often claimed that …
Everyone agrees that …	It is generally agreed that …
Opponents decided that …	It has been decided that …
People often assume that ….	It is often assumed that …

Different types of language to suit your purpose

To make your talk sound more persuasive you could also use any of the following.

Language/ rhetorical device	Effect/impact	Example
Rhetorical questions	These involve your audience and raise doubts or suggest undesirable alternatives.	*Is this what you would want for your pet? Would you allow your own children to eat that?*
Triple structures	This is one way to lodge ideas in your audience's mind through strong rhythmic patterns and suggest a range of options or benefits.	*This change would offer new jobs, new opportunities, a new life …* *… a chance for change, a chance for progress, a chance to make a real difference.*
Repetition	This is one way to reinforce ideas and lodge an idea in your audience's mind.	*Surely this is misguided. Surely this should stop.* *We need jobs, jobs and more jobs.*
Exclamations	These can add emotional weight and emphasis to your arguments.	*This practice must be stopped and quickly!* *So stop waiting and start acting!*
Emotive/evaluative language	This is a way to arouse emotions such as pity, anger or fear in your audience and add dramatic weight to your points.	– Loaded adjectives (eg, *slim* rather than *thin*; *devastating* rather than *harmful*; *ecstatic* rather than *happy*; *distraught* rather than *upset*; *grim* rather than *unpleasant*) – Powerful verbs (eg, *crammed* rather than *squashed*; *battered* rather than *hit*; *annihilated* rather than *defeated*; *smothered* rather than *covered*) – Bold statements such as: *"This is the stark and cruel reality of …", "Such a view is both naive and short-sighted."*
Exaggeration/ hyperbole	This can be used to discredit opponents' arguments. It can also provide a source of humour to gain your audience's interest and support.	*This seems to me about as sensible as fitting sliding doors on aeroplanes!*
Superlatives	This is a way to add weight and emphasis to points.	*There is no greater weapon to fight fear than ….* *The best approach is …* *The single most important factor …*

Language/ rhetorical device	Effect/impact	Example
Personal pronouns	Addressing your audience directly using "you" involves them in the presentation, while plural pronouns such as "we" and "us" help establish a connection with the audience and creates the impression that they are supporting you.	*Together we can make a change.* *Would you do this to your own home?* *So, let's start asking shop owners and suppliers where our clothes are made before we buy them.*
Subject-specific vocabulary	This can make you sound informed and knowledgeable about your topic. Avoid using too much technical language or jargon, which could confuse people who are not as familiar as you with the topic or issue.	Science—osmosis, photosynthesis English—oxymoron, metonymy Maths—polygon, quadratic Humanities—pyroclastic, alluvial Technology—CPU, worm, sprocket
Causal conjunctions	These are a way to help reinforce the logic of your arguments. Vary the position of these depending on how much emphasis you want to give the word. Place them at the front or near the front of your sentence or clause.	*It seems logical, **therefore**, to find an alternative.* ***So** next time you are out shopping, think carefully before buying …* ***Because** of this, many forests are disappearing.*
Comparative structures	These show you are not too narrow in your views and have considered opposing or alternative views. They allow you to address those views and then counter them with your own.	*While some may argue x, they ignore the fact that …* *While critics may claim x, recent evidence suggests …* *While opponents often highlight x, they fail to see …* *To those who suggest x, I would say …*
The language of facts	Highlights that you are basing your arguments on facts and evidence.	*A recent survey **proved** …* *Yesterday's poll **shows** …* *The investigation **revealed** …*
The language of opinion	Highlights that you are expressing your own view and taking a stand, or that others' arguments are merely opinions and not based on facts.	*Politicians **claim** that …* *People like me who **think** …* *Opponents have **suggested** that …* *Many proponents strongly **believe** that …* *Others **feel** that …*

Language/ rhetorical device	Effect/impact	Example
Lists of figures, types, quantities or numbers	These help add weight to your arguments.	*120 towns, 30,000 homes and over 1 million people*
Language expressing extremes	This is a way to add emphasis and impact to your points.	*There is **no doubt** that …* *It is **absolutely** clear that …* *It is **extremely** unlikely that …* *It seems **utterly** pointless to …*
Negative diction	This is a way to highlight problems or challenges.	*There is **no** easy solution.* ***None** of these efforts has made any improvements.* ***Not** a single government is in favour.* ***Neither** money **nor** new laws will change this.*
Modality/words that qualify	These words suggest possibility without making you sound like you are the authority on the topic.	*There are many who would **probably** agree.* *It **could** be argued that …* *Opponents **may** claim that …*
Verbs to show emphasis	These help make key points stand out.	Words such as: *emphasizes, highlights, reinforces, underlines, underscores, heightens, foregrounds, accentuates, etc.*
Syntax/word order	Reordering your sentences and clauses is one way to foreground certain words or ideas in the sentence and make them sound more prominent.	*What is totally unacceptable is …* *Devastated is how most tribal elders now feel … Deforestation is the biggest threat now facing …* *Action and a united approach are what we now need to help solve …*
Alliteration	This is a way to connect ideas and highlight words, and to lodge them in your audience's mind.	*Stopping now would be sheer stupidity.*
Hypotheticals	Showing your audience the alternative can persuade them to take action.	*Unless we act, and quickly, our children may never see tigers in the wild.*

PREPARING YOUR PRESENTATION

A key skill area in this section is information literacy. You will be learning about:

- **Selecting and organizing information**—identifying weaknesses, using primary and secondary sources, making connections between a variety of resources.
- **Referencing**—citing, footnotes and referencing sources, respecting the concept of intellectual property rights.

Key points that you will need to consider include the following.

- How will you organize your materials?
- How will you manage your time?
- How will you organize yourself or others (if working in a group)?
- What, if any, non-verbal aids will you use?

Organizing your materials

Having spent time planning your presentation, it is now time to prepare your materials. If you are working in a group you will need to think about how you might divide up the jobs here. For example, if working on a poster or a PowerPoint presentation you could split it up into sections to work on individually and then arrange for one person to collate everyone's material.

Managing your time

In Chapter 2 "The writing process" you read about ways to organize your time when writing an essay. When working in a group this is particularly important as you may need to work independently for some of the time. It is important to set clear time guidelines as you go.

ATL skills: organization

Organizing yourself or others

When preparing for a group presentation there are a number of roles and responsibilities you will need to negotiate right from the start through each phase of the presentation. Below are some of the issues you may need to address. See if you can think of any others.

Stages	Questions about group responsibilities
Planning	What are our individual interests, areas of expertise, knowledge and experience in relation to the topic and how can we best use them?
	How will we divide up the material for our topic to ensure we each play an equal role?
	How can we best manage our time and who will be responsible for keeping us on track?
Preparing	Who will prepare visual or other materials?
	Who will be responsible for collating our information?
	Who will be responsible for checking sources?
Practising	Where will we all stand?
	Who will operate technical devices?
	In which order will we present our material?
	How will we keep an eye on timings to ensure we each speak for more or less the same amount of time?
Presenting	Who will field questions?
	How will we transition from one speaker to the next?
	How will we monitor the volume and clarity of our speech?

Using visual and other aids

Always remember that you are being assessed on your speaking skills, not on the quality of your artwork or computer skills. First spend the time on what you are going to say—before committing time to designing colourful and interesting slides.

To avoid falling into this common trap, first ask yourself this question: "If I perform my presentation without any visual aids will anything be lost?" Think carefully about some of the following questions and consider how essential visual aids are to communicating your message.

- What will they add to your talk?
- Could they distract your audience?
- Can they be easily read by everyone in the room?
- Is the information presented in a clear and simple manner?

Having said that, visual aids can complement and benefit your presentation in several ways. For example, they can be helpful in providing **structure** to your presentation and in giving you cues to keep you on track.

Reasons to ban size zero models

- Encourages eating disorders

- Presents an unrealistic image of women

- Creates low self-esteem in young women

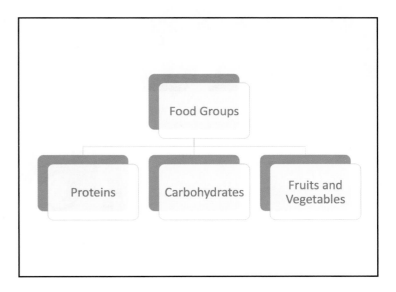

Visual aids can also help create an **emotional impact** on your audience. You have probably heard the expression, "A picture is worth a thousand words." This is something to consider when planning your presentation. Images are a powerful tool. An emotive picture can sometimes have a greater impact on your audience than your own words.

Images can also be helpful cues, **providing context** for members of your audience—and not only those who are second-language learners.

CHAPTER 5

Consider the following statements and the importance of visual aids in adding context.

When it came in from the wing it looked like he had misjudged the flight and wouldn't make any connection, but he brought it down beautifully before driving it home.

Trawling the net requires skill as much as experience.

An image defining a technical term, for example, can also be very helpful. A diagram explaining relationships or hierarchies can provide extra context and clarity for your listeners.

TIPS

If you have an important visual image or diagram, give your audience time to view and absorb it before talking. This will help ensure that when you begin talking to the image or diagram, you have their full attention.

Deciding on your presentation format

Using presentation programs

Technology offers ever more diverse and innovative ways to help you present your information. Before deciding on a program or package, it is important to think carefully about which format best suits your presentation and your audience. Software programs and packages such as PowerPoint and Prezi, which organize information in different ways (sequentially or switching between the bigger picture and the smaller details) may be one option, but you could also consider alternatives. You may choose to use a program such as Movie Maker or iMovie, which combines text, music, images and film clips, or insert a clip taken directly from the internet.

If you do decide to use visual aids or multimedia programmes and software, remember to avoid these common problems.

TIPS

Technology can be a powerful tool when used correctly but when misused can detract from your presentation. Remember, always ask yourself when considering using technology, "What will using technology add to my talk?" If the answer is little or nothing, you may be better off avoiding it.

Problem	Effect on audience	Suggested solution
Putting too much text on a slide	This encourages your audience to simply read off the slide rather than listen to you.	As a general rule aim for 36 words (6 lines of 6 words each) as a maximum.
Reading from your slides	This normally results from the mistake above. Once you start reading out your slide, your audience will do the same and stop listening to what you are saying.	Aim to include the basic ideas on your slide and use the slides as bullet points on which you can expand in your own words. Trust your own ability to use the slide as a cue card.
Using too many slides	Constant clicking can distract your audience and you may not give them enough time to absorb each slide.	Aim for no more than one slide every two minutes of your presentation.
Playing a clip from the internet with a slow internet connection	This can leave your audience waiting and result in a loss of interest and momentum in your presentation.	Always try to download the clip first to your computer and play it directly from there.
Using distracting movement and/or sound effects on the slides	This can slow down the presentation and again means the audience focuses on the slide and not on you or what you are saying.	Avoid using a range of different sounds or transitions. Keep them to a minimum and be sure you can upload your slide quickly if you are running out of time.
Using visuals that cannot easily be seen (font size, lack of contrast, inappropriate colours)	The audience will focus their efforts on trying to read the slide and will not listen to what you are saying.	Check your presentation is legible by standing at the back of the room and reading it before you begin.

Cue cards

Cue cards can be used as a tool to help you remember the order and structure of your talk. The key is to keep information to a minimum so that you are not tempted to read sentences from the cue card. A list of short bullet points of 3–5 words **each** is all you need.

Pet positives

a) Companionship (elderly)

b) Companionship (guide dogs)

c) Sense of security

d) Exercise for owner

e) Chance to meet others (with dogs)

Handouts

Handouts containing an outline of your presentation can be used, but be careful not to include everything or the audience will not wish to listen to your speech. Your handout could provide information about some useful sites with more information, the main points of your talk, as well as a space to write some notes. You could even mention the handout at the start to prevent people feeling a need to take notes, and hand it out at the end of your presentation.

Film clips

If you use a film clip, make sure to keep it brief to prevent losing the momentum of your talk. Once it has finished playing, make sure you comment on it and relate it directly to your talk. To avoid any embarrassing pauses or unnecessary interruptions to your presentation, ensure that the film clip is ready to play at the touch of a button. An interruption to sort out technical problems might mean your audience will switch off. This may mean you need to download the clip from the internet in advance.

web links

Check out this site for advice from Nancy Duarte on preparing and practising your presentation. http://blog.duarte.com/2011/02/10-ways-to-prepare-for-a-ted-format-talk/

PRACTISING YOUR PRESENTATION

This is an important stage in your presentation. You need to ensure that you allow time for a run-through in the planning stage of your presentation. This is the point at which you will find out where you can improve both the content and delivery of your material.

Communication

- **Informing others**—including presentation skills using a variety of media.
- **Giving and receiving feedback**—in a constructive way.

Collaboration

- **Working in groups**—including delegating and taking responsibility, adapting to roles, resolving group conflicts, demonstrating teamwork.
- **Accepting others**—analysing others' ideas, respecting others' points of view, using ideas critically.
- **Personal challenges**—negotiating goals and limitations with peers and with teachers.

Venue

If possible, try to practise in the venue you will be presenting in so that you are clear about the acoustics and space available. Try to use the same equipment if you have a computer or projector.

Audience

Try to have someone acting as an audience to offer constructive feedback and advice. If you cannot find anyone, you could video yourselves and try to see how you could improve. Analyse both the content and the delivery of your presentation.

ATL skill: reflection

Give the person acting as your audience a handout of your slides (6–9 slides per page) and ask them to note down what you say well (phrases that sound clear or make an impact) so that you can use them in the final presentation. Also make them identify things you did not communicate clearly.

TIPS

Content

You may discover that you repeat certain points in your talk, use language that is too technical, spend too long on certain points, or too little time on others. You may need clearer introductions to your points or transitions between them.

Delivery

You may realize things about your body language and speech that you were completely unaware of, for example, fidgeting with your hands. Or you may recognize a verbal filler you use in your speech (saying "um" or "er"), or that you overuse a certain word or phrase. With practice and someone's supervision you can help eliminate these.

Timing

Check your timings with a stopwatch to ensure you do not run over the allotted time for your presentation. If working in a group, it is important to make sure that you all stick to timelines.

Be wary of building in time for questions. Very often these can take up a lot of your time as your questioners may make mini-speeches themselves rather than asking a quick question.

Make sure you do not rush your talk because your time is short. You may give the impression that you are nervous, and you want to avoid doing that.

Positioning

As a general rule it is easier to stand still. This will avoid distracting your audience. However, if you are working in a group you may need to move about, depending upon the space. Think about where you are going to stand and how you can clearly direct the audience's attention at the speaker and avoid having others distract the audience's attention from the person talking.

Transitions

Think about how you will switch between sections of your talk and/or between different speakers. Will each speaker introduce the next person or will you step forwards/backwards when talking? To save time and to appear confident and organized, you should aim to move seamlessly between presenters. This takes practice.

Predict questions or problems

Another useful strategy is to try to predict any questions you may be asked following your talk. If you are delivering a persuasive talk, think of counter-arguments. Practising your talk in front of family or friends should raise any questions you may have to deal with, and it offers you the chance to receive feedback from someone whose opinion you value and trust.

Avoid reading at all costs

As soon as you begin reading from a paper:

- your eyes lower and you lose eye contact with your audience
- your head lowers so your voice does not project outwards
- your voice becomes more monosyllabic as you focus on decoding the words on the paper rather than thinking about your tone and pitch.

PRESENTING

The key to a successful presentation is engaging your audience. Too often students focus more on the content and not enough on how they will present it. Making your delivery interesting and effective requires thought and practice. You may want to consider the following questions.

- How will you dress (formally or informally)?
- Where will you stand (in one place or moving about)?
- What body language will you adopt (eye contact, gestures, facial expression)?
- How will you use your voice effectively to engage your audience?
- How will you incorporate your visual aids?

TIPS

Be adaptable!

Practising your presentation will nearly always raise issues for improvement. Do not be afraid to make changes (removing or adding material) if you think it will help you produce a clearer, more engaging and convincing presentation.

ATL skills: communication, collaboration

TIPS

One good way to remember the key elements to a successful delivery of your presentation is to think of the **"Seven Cs"**.

Make eye **C**ontact.
Sound **C**onfident.
Be **C**lear.
Sound **C**onvincing.

Be **C**oncise.
Be **C**ourteous.
Show you **C**are about your topic.

Eye contact

Make sure you look up and make as much eye contact as you can with your audience. This will help make your speech seem more confident and convincing. It will also allow you to see if your audience are interested and awake!

In addition to making eye contact with individual people in the audience, try sweeping your eyes across faces in the crowd looking for frowns, confused expressions or shaking heads. Be prepared to notice these so that you can ask your audience questions such as, "I can see that what I have said doesn't quite gel with you, so do you have a question you would like to ask?". This will enable you to clarify points for those who are confused or in disagreement.

Your voice

How you say it is as important as **what** you say. If no one can hear you your entire presentation is a waste of time. You could be providing the most incredible information about a new scientific space discovery but if no one can hear you, you may as well be talking about your shopping!

Vary your pace. It is important to speak slowly in order to allow your audience time to process what you are saying. When you are nervous you tend to speak faster. Aim to talk at half your normal speed. You also need to slow down when making key points. Pausing for effect is a crucial skill and can be used at key points to add emphasis and impact to your message.

Speak clearly and confidently. It is important to enunciate your words and avoid mumbling. The more confident you sound, the more likely you will be to persuade your listeners.

Project your voice. It is important to speak loudly enough so that you can be heard by everyone in the room. Be sure to ask your audience at the outset if everyone can hear you, or have a friend at the back of the room signal to you if you need to speak louder.

Vary your expression and pitch. This will add variety to your voice and help maintain your audience's interest. Speaking more softly in places will force your audience to listen. With stress and intonation you can also emphasize important words or phrases (for example, "A *key* point here is . . .", "There are *three* main reasons for . . .").

Sound enthusiastic. It is important that you sound interested in the material you are presenting—even if you are not! If you sound disinterested your audience will certainly not be captivated by your talk.

Control your body language. Think about how you will stand, what gestures you will use.

web links

Check out this site to see how you can use body language to emphasize what you are saying. http://changingminds.org/techniques/body/emphasis_body.htm

Be aware of your positioning. Avoid moving about too much as this will distract your audience. Be sure to stand where you can face all of your audience and where you avoid blocking any visual aids you may be using.

Take care of your appearance. First impressions can influence the audience's attitudes to you. Dress appropriately for the occasion.

ACTIVITY

TACTICS FOR TALKS

Discuss the following options with a partner and decide which advice is most suitable for various types of presentation.

Avoid eye contact.
Look at your audience.
Dress smartly.
Dress casually.
Smile.
Look serious.
Stand in one place.
Move around.
Use gestures to add impact.
Keep your arms by your side.

ATL skills: communication

Time: 5 minutes

Pairs

web links

For more useful tips and hints on presenting, visit this site.

http://lorien.ncl.ac.uk/ming/dept/tips/present/comms.htm

Below is a checklist you could refer to for delivery of your presentation.

- [ ] Appear confident and in control when you stand up. Expect success!
- [ ] Begin strongly and make an impact.
- [ ] Do not read—use prompts but know your key ideas and expand on your notes.
- [ ] Look up—face your audience **at all times** and make eye contact to check their engagement.
- [ ] Use gestures to involve the audience and emphasize key points—be animated.
- [ ] Think about your posture and body language—look confident and enthused.
- [ ] Vary your expression—sound interested, engaged and enthused.
- [ ] Project your voice; speak loudly, slowly and clearly; enunciate your words.
- [ ] Use formal language (for example, "children", not "kids") at all times.
- [ ] Ensure smooth changeovers between presenters.
- [ ] End strongly—know your conclusions and end with a clear statement that makes an impact. Don't let your presentation drift off to a weak close.
- [ ] Be persuasive. Convince us! Sound convinced about your own material.
- [ ] Stand still when other members in your group are presenting.

When delivering your presentation, remember that **your job is to persuade and convince your audience** to believe and agree with what you are saying.

LEARNING FROM THE EXPERTS

ATL skills: reflection, thinking

Below are some famous public speeches by men and women from all walks of life. Read or watch them and see how many strategies and techniques mentioned in this chapter you can find.

"Stay Hungry, Stay Foolish". Steve Jobs. http://www.youtube.com/watch?v=UF8uR6Z6KLc	"Farewell to Baseball". Lou Gherig. http://www.ranker.com/list/famous-short-speeches/william-neckard
"54th EMMY Awards". Oprah Winfrey. http://www.famousquotes.me.uk/speeches/Oprah-Winfrey/index.htm	"Women's Rights". Hillary Clinton. http://www.famousquotes.me.uk/speeches/Hillary-Clinton/index.htm
"I Have a Dream". Martin Luther King Jr. http://www.americanrhetoric.com/speeches/mlkihaveadream.htm	"Afghanistan Speech". Tony Blair. http://www.putlearningfirst.com/language/20rhet/blair.html
"Gettysburg Address". Abraham Lincoln. http://www.ranker.com/list/famous-short-speeches/william-neckard	"Landmines Speech". Princess Diana. http://www.famousquotes.me.uk/speeches/Princess-Diana/index.htm
"Schools Kill Creativity". TED talk. Sir Ken Robinson. www.ted.com/talks/ken_robinson_says_schools_kill_creativity.html	Find one of your own!

TIPS

You have daily opportunities to see people presenting in school. Watch your teachers and fellow students and think about what makes their teaching or their talk memorable. Think of ways to use their strategies and styles in your presentation.

A FINAL WORD OF ADVICE

One of the biggest hurdles to students' success in presentations is the fear of standing up in front of an audience. Below are several steps and tips you could use to overcome the fear of making a mistake or looking foolish when you speak to a group.

- Be well-prepared before speaking to a group.
- Practise your speech—talk to friends, to family and people you trust or feel comfortable with and who will give you frank and constructive advice.
- Relax yourself just before you speak by taking deep breaths.
- Have a backup (such as cue cards) in case you forget what you want to say.
- Focus on your audience rather than yourself, which will divert your attention away from your own anxieties.
- Try to enjoy it—presenting well can be enormously rewarding and very often the audience will be keen to hear what you have to say!
- Sound interested in your topic and try to model the response that you want your audience to have to what you say.

web links

For more useful tips and hints, visit these sites.

http://www.impactfactory.com/gate/public_speaking_training_course/freegate_1552-1104-88327.html

http://www.ehow.com/way_5245401_good-oral-presentation_.html

http://courseweb.fst.edu/pryds/study/presentation.pdf

http://www.rogerdarlington.me.uk/Speech.html

http://www.rogerdarlington.me.uk/Presentation.htm

http://sourcedaddy.com/ms-powerpoint/common-powerpoint-problems-and-solutions.html

KEY POINTS OF THE CHAPTER

ATL skills

- Organization
- Communication
- Thinking
- Collaboration
- Transfer
- Information literacy

The four main stages of producing a presentation

- Planning
- Preparing
- Practising
- Presenting

Don't forget

- Make your talk CRISP.
- Remember the "Seven Cs".
- Be adaptable to making changes.
- Only use technology if it adds something to your presentation.
- Watch other people give talks and learn from them.
- Use rhetorical devices in moderation.

Useful websites

http://prezi.com/. This is a presentation site that allows you to move smoothly and seamlessly between the big picture and small details.

Useful presentation tips can be found at the following sites:

http://blog.duarte.com/2011/02/10-ways-to-prepare-for-a-ted-format-talk/

http://changingminds.org/techniques/body/emphasis_body.htm

http://courseweb.fst.edu/pryds/study/presentation.pdf

http://www.ehow.com/way_5245401_good-oral-presentation_.html

http://www.impactfactory.com/gate/public_speaking_training_course/freegate_1552-1104-88327.html

http://lorien.ncl.ac.uk/ming/dept/tips/present/comms.htm

http://www.magma.ca/~waisvisz/mytips.htm

http://www.naturaltraining.com/training/presentation-skills/

http://www.plu.edu/libr/media/designing_visuals.html

http://www.powertopresent.com

http://www.rogerdarlington.me.uk/Speech.html

http://www.rogerdarlington.me.uk/Presentation.htm

http://sourcedaddy.com/ms-powerpoint/common-powerpoint-problems-and-solutions.html

http://www.ted.com/talks/nancy_duarte_the_secret_structure_of_great_talks.html.

The following sites contain graphic organizers that can help you with the planning of your presentation:

http://edhelper.com/teachers/graphic_organizers.htm

http://www.realclassroomideas.com/resources/graphic+organizers-oralpresentationnotecard.pdf (for cue cards)

http://www.enchantedlearning.com/graphicorganizers/ (for visual aids as well)

http://www.eduplace.com/kids/hme/k_5/graphorg/

http://www.k111.k12.il.us/lafayette/fourblocks/graphic_organizers.htm

http://www.teach-nology.com/worksheets/graphic/ (for a good list)

http://www.region15.org/curriculum/graphicorg.html

http://www.graphic.org/goindex.html

http://www.sdcoe.k12.ca.us/score/actbank/torganiz.htm

References

Gibbons, P. 2002. *Scaffolding Language, Scaffolding Learning: Teaching Second-Language Learners in the Mainstream Classroom*. Portsmouth, New Hampshire, USA. Heinemann.

International Baccalaureate. 2008. *MYP: From principles into practice.* Cardiff, UK. International Baccalaureate.

Polias, J. 2000. *Language and Literacy: Classroom applications of functional grammar*. Adelaide, South Australia: Department of FEE.

Seims, R. (ed). 1996. *Teaching Language Secondary*. Victoria, AU. Curriculum Corporation.

CHAPTER 6

OBJECTIVES

In this chapter you will learn:

- which ATL skills will support you best in studying and preparing well for tests, exams and all assessments.

Within those skill groups you will also learn the specific skills you need to:

- generate the motivation you need to help you with your studies
- create an effective study timetable that you will stick to
- overcome procrastination
- create good notes in class and for your studies at home
- set up your home study environment for maximum effectiveness—including what music to use and what foods to eat to help you concentrate
- overcome any examination nerves, and
- use good exam-room techniques.

This chapter is specifically related to passing tests and exams but some of the ideas will help you with all your studying throughout the year. In this chapter there are lots of activities for you to do, so you will need a piece of paper and a pen beside you while you read. This chapter can be worked through at any time of the year but would be most useful between 8 and 10 weeks before a major test, an exam or a deadline for a major project or piece of work.

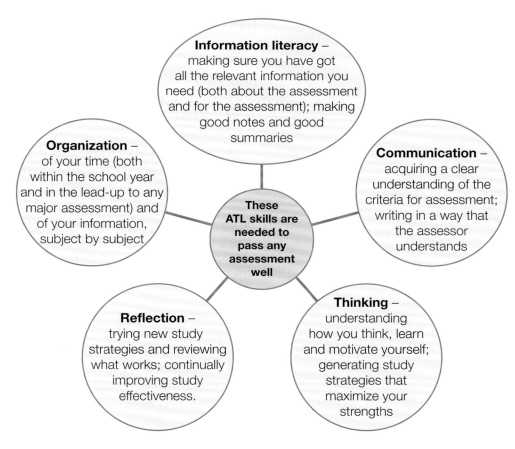

Information literacy – making sure you have got all the relevant information you need (both about the assessment and for the assessment); making good notes and good summaries

Organization – of your time (both within the school year and in the lead-up to any major assessment) and of your information, subject by subject

Communication – acquiring a clear understanding of the criteria for assessment; writing in a way that the assessor understands

These ATL skills are needed to pass any assessment well

Reflection – trying new study strategies and reviewing what works; continually improving study effectiveness.

Thinking – understanding how you think, learn and motivate yourself; generating study strategies that maximize your strengths

MOTIVATION TO STUDY

Motivation is the thing that spurs you on to study, but it is also the thing that is hardest to maintain. Ask yourself the following questions.

- What comes first in the whole study process?
- What leaves first in the whole study process?

Is the answer **motivation**?

OK then, let's start with that.

Think about the purpose of assessments, assignments, tests and exams. What are they for?

- To make you suffer?
- To criticize your work?
- To keep you busy so that you can't get into mischief?
- To give you an opportunity to build up points that will get you closer to finishing this year successfully?
- To provide an opportunity for you to fail?

Or

- To create an opportunity for you to learn something well?
- To give you feedback on how your learning is progressing so far?
- To give you a chance to test yourself, to find out what you are capable of?
- To enable you to become a more effective learner through the practice of good study skills?
- To provide an opportunity for you to shine?

Your motivation is shaped by your perspective—the things that you decide to focus on will shape the way you feel. If you view all assessments negatively, then it is much harder for you to do your best work.

If you deliberately take a positive perspective, then you will find you can:

- relax more
- think more clearly
- organize more efficiently
- come up with great ideas, and
- produce better work.

This is the secret of motivation, the big secret, the secret that is so secret that it might shock you …

You have a choice.

It might seem like a bit of an anticlimax, but that's it. You have a choice:

- in everything that you think and feel
- in your reaction or response to anything that ever happens to you
- in interpreting any situation or any event that you ever face.

So you can choose to see assessments of all kinds as being unfair punishments imposed upon you by the education system, or you can see them as opportunities to learn, to grow, to improve, to shine, to be brilliant.

It's up to you.

Remember, your perspective shapes your motivation.

Motivation is simply the drive that you have naturally when you are engaged in doing something you love. It might be when you are playing sport or it could be when you're singing or painting or acting or playing Xbox or skating or surfing or skiing or reading or writing or something else. When you are doing the thing that you enjoy most, do you notice how much energy you have, how well you focus and how well you learn new things? That's the power of what's called internal or **intrinsic** motivation—the power to put in huge amounts of effort, to persist and persevere even when the going gets hard, the power to try and keep trying, the power never to give up.

Intrinsic: means within yourself, inside, as opposed to extrinsic, which means outside yourself.

Now just imagine what you could achieve, academically, if you could apply that same kind of motivational power to your school work!

Of course, when you are doing the things you enjoy most, it seems like this motivational power happens by itself. Suddenly you find you are stretching yourself, able to concentrate, to try harder, to put in effort, to learn from mistakes and persevere without even thinking about it.

However, when you are doing something that you don't enjoy so much—maybe studying or doing homework—those same abilities might not switch on so easily. You have to turn them on yourself, that's the trick. When you are faced with something that you need to do but don't particularly want to do, you still have all those amazing abilities available to you—you just have to learn how to switch them on, deliberately, on purpose when you need them most, to generate a motivated state.

ACTIVITY

ATL skills: thinking, reflection

 Time: 10 minutes

 Individual or class

PERSONAL MOTIVATION STRATEGY

Think of a time when you managed to do something that you thought was going to be difficult. A time when you faced a challenge and overcame it. When you weren't sure you were going to get it done but you managed to get it done anyway.

Now write down how you managed to overcome the difficulty. You knew it was going to be hard so how did you get yourself to give it a go anyway?

What did you do?

Notice that you already know how to motivate yourself in the way that this chapter has been discussing. You already know how to get yourself to do hard stuff. Whatever you wrote down is one of your own ways to do that—a self-motivational strategy that works for you.

Motivation strategies

Examples of different strategies include:

- talking to yourself in a particular way—using specific words to self-motivate or to convince yourself
- imagining the goal is already achieved
- describing to yourself how you are going to tackle this hard thing and then encouraging yourself as you work through it
- starting before you have time to back out
- spontaneous impulse—the "just do it" approach.

Every person is different.

All you have to do in order to generate the motivation you need to get your studying and homework done is to notice how you've done it before, when you've needed to, and copy that process. But this time **do it deliberately**.

Once you have mastered that, all you need are some good strategies to make sure that all your newfound motivation, determination and effort are put to good use.

The key thing that marks out the best students in the world is their ability to apply their most effective learning and thinking strategies when they need them—whether it is in a situation they enjoy or not. They know that success at school comes from using the right learning strategies—the ones that work for them.

To do this, of course, you need a lot of learning strategies to choose from—a **learning strategy library**, in fact—and that is what this chapter is for. To give you lots of study and learning strategies to choose from.

Let's start with the most obvious ones.

ACTIVITY

ATL skills: thinking, reflection

Time: 10 minutes

Individual or class

WHAT WORKS AND WHAT DOESN'T WORK

Think back to your last piece of assessed work—this could be an assignment, test or exam—and then think back further to your whole history of completing different assessments.

Think about the things that you do in leading up to assessments and write them down in two lists.

- List 1: All the things that, on reflection, you think were useful things for you to do—things that helped you with the assessment.
- List 2: All the things that were not so useful.

See if you can come up with five things in each list.

List 1 The things I did that worked

- I planned well ahead.
- I made good notes.
- I asked the teachers extra questions for clarity.
- Etc …

List 2 The things I did that didn't work

- I didn't take it seriously enough.
- I left it all to the last minute.
- I watched too much TV.
- Etc …

After making your own list, compare it with other people in your class to see if there are differences.

Your first list is the start of your **learning strategy library** and the second list shows the things you need to work on.

Did your second list contain any of the following?

- I left it to the last minute.
- I kept putting it off.
- I procrastinated.

ORGANIZATION

Remember, the **solution** to procrastination is **organization**.

Making a full-year assessment timetable

This is an exercise that will help you overcome procrastination (your tendency to put things off until the last minute) by showing you how to organize yourself so that you complete all your assignments without a rush or last-minute panic.

ACTIVITY

ATL skills: organization

 Time: 30 minutes to 1 hour

  Individual or class

MAKING A FULL-YEAR ASSESSMENT TIMETABLE

1. Get yourself a big year planner or wallchart with room to write in something every day.
2. Mark in all the important dates for the year—the term start/end dates, any midterm breaks, national holidays, the most important sports or other performance dates for you and any exam dates.
3. Get all your assignment dates for the rest of the year from all your teachers—both the start and completion dates—and mark them in.

In order to complete part 3 of this activity you must have the cooperation of your teachers, who will need to be this organized as well.

When you are working on an assignment or project, you will probably find that these are the main stages you will need to complete.

a. Finding the information—research
b. Processing the information—reading
c. Planning the piece of work—sequencing ideas
d. Doing the work
e. Proofing, making final changes and handing it in

How would you divide your time between the different stages?

Here's an estimate of the average split of time spent on each stage (as a percentage). You can adjust this to suit your own situation.

Stage 1: Research	25%
Stage 2: Reading	25%
Stage 3: Planning	5%
Stage 4: Doing the work	40%
Stage 5: Proofing	5%

Once you have all your assignment completion dates from your teachers, and you have marked them on your year planner, you can then create a timeline for every assignment. You do this by marking in the dates prior to completion of each assignment when you will need to have finished each of stages 1 to 5—give each stage a completion date for each assignment.

Aim always to finish assignments with at least one day to spare.

Making an exam (test, major assessment) study timetable

This exercise will focus on helping you plan your study time prior to an exam or major test but could also be used for planning your time for the completion of a major project. It is designed to help you organize all your study time over a short time period—up to 8 weeks before the deadline.

ACTIVITY

ATL skills: organization

Time: 30 minutes to 1 hour

Individual or class

YOUR STUDY TIMETABLE

This time you only need a calendar that runs from eight weeks **before** your first major exam/assessment date to the end of your last assessment/exam.

Get one, make one, find one, print one out.

Now just follow these steps and make sure you complete each step before you move on to the next step.

1. **Mark in all the calendar dates.**
    Highlight weekends, holidays, study-break days before the exams, maybe all in different colours.
2. **Mark in all your important events.**
    Include every examination and the time when you have to be there; sports or games; any competitions or performances; any days where you would not expect to be able to do any study at all because of other equally important events.
3. **Take out one day a week.**
    In the eight weeks before your first exam, make sure you have one day each week where you are not going to do any study at all—that day might be one of the days marked out in Step 2, or you might choose another day. Remember, select only one day per week, and then cross it out. The advantage of starting exam study early is that you have a bit of time to relax.

TIPS

Remember:

It is not for the rest of your life. It's only for this short period of time!

4. **Write in on every available day how much time you are prepared to commit to study on that day.**
   a. Decide how much and write it in on the timetable: 1, 1½, 2, 5, 8 hours per day (whatever you think you can do per day). Remember that on a weekend day or a holiday you can fit in a lot more hours of study than on a school day.
   b. After any exam don't give yourself more than half a day recovery time. Get back into your study as soon as you can, ready for the next exam. Keep up the rhythm until it is all completely over.
   c. Make sure you do some study every possible day, and make the amount of time realistic.
   d. Anything less than half an hour of study on any one day is going to be a waste of time. Any more than eight hours of study on any one day might be too much.

5. **Add up your total study time.**
   a. Add up all the hours you have just written in.
   b. For a study timetable covering 8 weeks prior to a serious exam, fewer than 20 hours might not be serious enough and more than 200 hours might be too much. But remember, everyone is different.

6. **Prioritize all your subjects.**
   a. Prioritize your assessable/exam subjects starting with the subject that will take the most time and effort, working towards the one that will take the least.
   b. If you have any non-examination subjects that still require you to invest considerable time at the same time of year in order to prepare work for assessment (for example, preparing your portfolio for art or design technology) include those subjects in your list as well.
   c. If you have the results from your "mock" exams, then use those results to work out which subjects you need to spend the most time on.

7. **Divide up your total study time between all the subjects on your list.**
   a. Give more hours to the subjects at the top of the list and fewer hours to each subject further down the list.
   b. Make sure that the hours still add up to the total study time calculated in Step 5.

8. **Allocate all subjects to days in your timetable in chunks of 1–2 hours.**
    a. Take the subject at the top of your list (for example, chemistry: 22 hours) and break those 22 hours up across your timetable in chunks of 1–2 hours, then do the same for every subject.
    b. Make sure you allocate some time every week to each subject.
    c. Most students find it is best to avoid spending less than 1 hour or more than 4 hours at a time on any one subject, but that is a personal thing. You need to work out what works best for you.
    d. There is one exception to the advice in Step 8c above—on the day before any exam make sure you only study that one subject for the whole of the day.
    e. For most students it works best to focus on getting depth into your study, rather than covering a little of each subject each night.
9. **Colour code it.**
    a. Once you have finished, go back and colour code your subjects and highlight the actual exam times in different colours too.
    b. Make it look good and pin it on the wall in the place where you study.

Now you have a timetable—all you have to do is stick to it.

Calculating a study rate

This last exercise aims to help you make sure you have enough time to get through all the work that you need to do in each subject.

You need to estimate how much work in total you want to get through in your study, then divide that by the hours you have allocated for study, and finally work out some kind of study rate for each subject.

ACTIVITY

ATL skills: organization

 Time: 15 minutes

  Individual or class

CALCULATING YOUR STUDY RATE

1. For each subject, count the total number of topics (or pages or assessment standards) that you want to cover in your study and divide that number by the study hours available for that subject.

For example: mathematics—20 topics and 10 hours available means a study rate of 2 topics per hour.

Calculate a study rate for each subject.

2. Check and adjust your study time based on your study rate.

Once you have a study rate to aim at in each subject, you can check whether you are meeting that rate. If you are not, either add extra hours of study into your timetable for that subject or, if you are exceeding the study rate, take time out.

3. Make the timetable a living document.

If there are any changes at all to your timetabled hours due to unexpected events, make the changes on your timetable.

Move hours around to make sure you still achieve your targets.

That's the solution to procrastination!

Give yourself a deadline every day throughout the study and exam period, and try to stick to each one.

TIPS

If you miss a scheduled study time, don't panic! Move the hours you should have done to another part of your timetable. Stick to your targets.

USING YOUR BRAIN WELL

Your brain

The parts of the brain that you mostly use for thinking are arranged in two hemispheres—the left and the right.

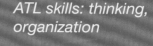

ATL skills: thinking, organization

Each hemisphere specializes in a different type of thinking.

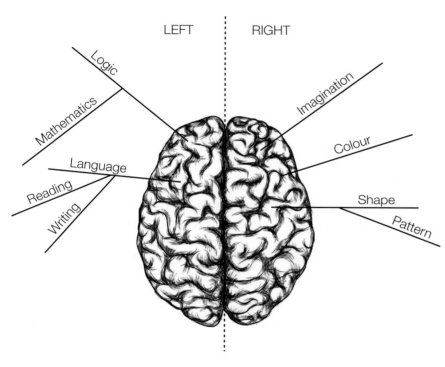

These two types of thinking can be thought of as "thinking in words" and "thinking without words".

Do you ever notice that sometimes you are talking to yourself inside your head (practising self-talk) while you're doing something, and other times you are not?

THINKING

Thinking that requires self-talk:
- thinking about what you are going to say to someone
- singing a song to yourself
- while you are reading
- while you are writing
- having "internal conversations".

Thinking that does not require self-talk:
- thinking in pictures, sounds that aren't words, tastes, smells, skin sensations, movement, emotion
- when drawing, painting, sculpting, designing
- when immersed in music (either playing or listening)
- daydreaming.

Word processing is almost exclusively handled by two areas of the brain—**Wernicke's** area and **Broca's** area—which in most people (95% of right-handed people and 70% of left-handed people) are both located in the left hemisphere of the brain.

Mental processing without words—pictures, shapes, patterns, colour, imagination—seems to happen more in the right hemisphere of the brain. In the other 5% of right-handed people and the other 30% of left-handed people there seems to be a complete swap of the functioning of the hemispheres.

But where this thinking happens is not that relevant—the important thing is that we all have two distinct thinking styles operating in our heads all the time. It is important when we are trying to learn new things that we involve both types of thinking all the time in order to make the best use of the whole of our brain.

Note-making

To involve the whole of your brain (and both types of thinking) when you are making notes, just follow this simple procedure.

Take a whole, normal clean page that you are intending to write notes on.

Each night, read notes, pull out main ideas and put them here.

Write class notes here.

Change colours for each new idea.

1. Before you write your notes, whether in class or at home, draw a vertical line down the page about one third of the way across the page from the left side (right-handers) or from the right side (left-handers).
2. Only write your notes on the two-thirds side of the page.

If you are writing all your notes only in blue or black, and if there are no pictures or diagrams or imagination involved, then the part of the brain that processes without words will have nothing to focus on, will get bored and will probably take you off into daydreaming. To keep all of your brain focused on what you are learning and what you are writing, follow Step 3.

3. Change colours each time the information you are writing changes to a new idea. Your class notes will end up being more interesting and every idea will be separated from every other idea by colour, making your notes easier to read.

The other part is the column on the left (or right)—this is for your summary points. If you want to understand and remember the information you receive in class you **must** go over it again within 24 hours of seeing it for the first time. This is to do with memory. One thing we know for sure about memory is that information that is only seen once is very hard to remember. If you want to remember what you have written in class, follow Step 4.

4. Each night read through the notes you wrote that day in class, pull out the key points (the main ideas) and put them in as a summary in the column on the left (or right), as words or pictures or a table or a graph.

Brain music

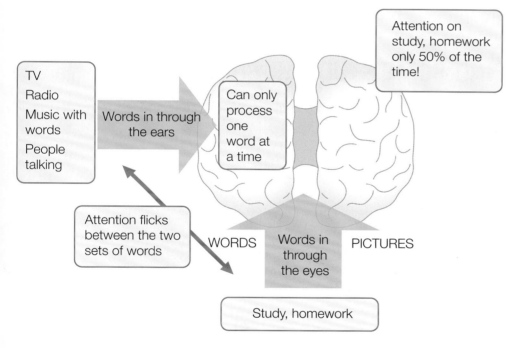

One thing we know for sure about the word processing part of our brain is that it can only process one word at a time. It can do that very quickly—but still, only one word at a time. Have you ever noticed in class when you are copying down written information from the board and the teacher tries to explain it to you out loud at the same time, you get confused? What is happening is that your brain is flicking backwards and forwards between the words you are seeing and the words you are hearing, and you can easily lose track.

If you ever study with the TV or the radio on, or with **music with words** playing, you are doing the same thing to yourself. Your brain will try to pay some attention to both sets of words—those you are seeing and those you are hearing.

This means your brain is only paying attention to your study or homework 50% of the time. You are only working at half speed!

If you want to double the amount of information you can process in the same amount of time—and double the amount you can remember of what you study—turn off the TV, the radio, your favourite music, sign out of chat, or anything that involves extra processing in words. This will then enable your brain to process the words of your study or homework with 100% efficiency.

However, you don't have to study in absolute silence if you don't want to. All you have to do is find some music you like **that has no words**. Instrumental music is brilliant for study, as long as it is something you like listening to. All sorts of instrumental music work well—jazz, piano, guitar music, movie soundtracks. Even dance music works well, as long as it is not too loud. If you like it, many forms of classical music work well too.

ACTIVITY

ATL skills: information literacy, thinking

 Time: 10 minutes

  Individual

FIND SOME STUDY MUSIC

Go online or into your music collection and find some instrumental music that you like.

Posture terrible, taking full body weight on muscles

Light directly above putting work into shadow

Stressed, tired student defeated before you start

Chair too low, desk too low

Study space

Right now you might get all your homework and any study done lying on the floor or on your bed, but the higher you go in the education system the more time you will need to spend sitting at a desk or table engaged in writing or working on a keyboard.

Relaxed, focused student, more energy, more persistence

Light onto the page

Chair high enough for good posture – supporting full weight on skeleton.

Desk high enough to allow writing and keyboard work without leaning

Brain food

There are three key foods for your brain.

- **Oxygen**—a 5-minute movement break after every 45 minutes of study to re-oxygenate your brain
- **Fruit**—for energy, instead of high-sugar foods
- **Water**—plain water for hydrating

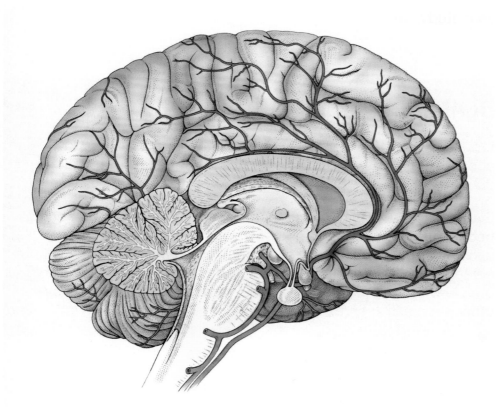

Dealing with distractions

Do you ever find that when you are at home in the evening and you start thinking about getting some study or homework done, what pops into your mind instantly are thoughts of all the things you want to do more than studying? Do you find you start thinking about all the other things you could be doing until it becomes really distracting and suddenly you find yourself in front of the TV or the computer or on your phone and you discover that you have put off the school work until later? Or are you one of those people who can get rid of such distracting thoughts and get down to working when you need to?

The other types of distractions that can constantly interfere with you getting your work done are of the personal maintenance kind. Do you ever find that when you need to get some study done, you suddenly get the urge to tidy your room or do the dishes, etc? These are things you are doing in order to delay getting started, and so these personal maintenance things need to be all sorted out before you begin. Similarly, your need to get snacks, water, tissues, slippers, a hairclip, comfortable clothes, go to the bathroom, etc all need to be sorted out **before** you start your study.

ACTIVITY

ATL skills: reflection, thinking

 Time: 5–20 minutes

 Whole class

DEALING WITH DISTRACTIONS

Write down some ways that you deal with distracting thoughts about other things you could be doing when you need to study or do homework.

Everyone suffers from this problem but research shows that some people have a strategy—a secret way of turning distractions into something that actually helps to keep them focused and persevering until the task is done—and other people don't. The people who have learned this secret have a huge advantage over other people in everything they do.

CASE STUDY

Delayed gratification

At Stanford University in the 1960s a psychologist named Walter Mischel created an experiment that he ran with 4-year-old children from the local crèche. He set up interviews between these children, one at a time, and an adult researcher. The researcher would ask each child a few questions that they could easily answer and when they were finished he would take a marshmallow out of his pocket and put it on the table in front of the child as a reward for them. He would then tell them that they could eat it straight away if they wanted to, but he was going to go out of the room for a few minutes and when he came back, if they hadn't eaten it, then they would get another marshmallow as well. If the marshmallow had been eaten the child would get no more.

Then the researcher went away, leaving the 4-year-old in the room on their own—just one child and one marshmallow. The researcher didn't stay away for just a minute or two, he stayed away for a long time (up to 20 minutes). Also, the children did not realize they were being observed throughout this time by psychologists behind mirrored glass.

Now, of course, some of the kids ate the marshmallow straight away but some of them didn't. Some of them went to great lengths to keep from eating the marshmallow—talking strictly to themselves, covering their eyes with their hands, hiding under the table or in the corner of the room. Doing whatever they could to keep themselves from eating the first marshmallow. Finally, the researcher did come back. If the marshmallow was gone the child was allowed to leave, but if the marshmallow was still there, untouched, the child got another marshmallow and then was allowed to leave.

So they ended up with two groups—those that grabbed and those that held out.

These two groups were then followed up for many years afterwards and were tested in every way possible. The results were compared between the two groups.

Now the results that they obtained were very significant because in every test as these kids grew up, the group that had held out did better. They were:

- more academically competent—30% higher test results
- better able to concentrate and learn
- better at setting goals and achieving them
- more socially competent
- better at handling challenges
- more self-reliant, confident, trustworthy and dependable
- better at taking the initiative and less likely to stress, regress or give up in the face of difficulties.

Later in life these two groups were measured again and the "hold out" group were found to have been much more successful in life in general. They were much happier and had an income, on average, double that of the other group.

Now the point of the story is not what you think **you** might have done as a 4-year-old in that situation. The point is simply that one of the best measures of our ability to create success for ourselves is **whether we have learned how to put off pleasure in order to get the work done**. Not to deny pleasure, but to delay it in order to get the work done. This is called **delayed gratification**.

The secret to handling distractions, if they are thoughts of some of the pleasurable things in your life, is to say to yourself, "Yes, I will have that, I will watch TV or YouTube or spend time texting my friends or on Facebook, **but** I will have it **after** I get my work done. As a reward for my efforts."

For the weeks leading up to your exams, you need to make study the **highest priority** in your life, and have your enjoyment second. Not for the rest of your life, but just for the next few weeks until your exams are over. Nothing should be more important than your study.

HOW DO YOU STUDY?

In Chapter 1 "Learning about learning", we said the two most important things to remember about study are:

1. if you don't know how to study effectively, then you are not alone—it is not a subject that is often taught in schools
2. the best students in the world use a variety of study strategies and they continually modify their ways of study to suit their subjects and their school system.

So if you learn how to study well you will have a huge advantage.

First, you have to understand things well—topic by topic, idea by idea.

Next, you have to put all your understandings together within any one subject in order to get the coherence and flow you need to apply and transfer the information.

Understanding and organizing information

In order to understand things well you need good information, and you need someone available to explain things when you don't understand the information.

1. Good information—this means taking proper notes in class and having quality textbooks.
2. Available explanations—this requires teachers to be available for you when you have a problem or a question.

If I don't understand something the first place I go to get some clarity is YouTube. The good thing about YouTube is that it is not commercial, it is amateur and clips of school subjects are there because someone thought they might help. The other good thing is that it is visual. Most people pick up much more information from a visual presentation than they do from any auditory one. Pick a topic, any topic and you will find a huge number of clips explaining it to you, scan through them until you find one you like. It is so easy. For example, one of the most essential things to understand if you are studying chemistry is valency—electrons and atoms and why one thing bonds with another. Go to YouTube and look up valency—the clips are great.

If you have good information and you have used all the resources you can find and you still don't understand something, you need to discuss it with your teacher or find an expert and ask them or get some extra tuition organized with an older student or a specialist after-school tutor.

Once you have got all the information you need, you then have to process it.

How are you going to do that? Read, and reread and reread?

In the "What works and what doesn't work" activity earlier in this chapter you were asked to list some of the things you had done in the past that had helped you pass your assessments and some of the things you had done that didn't help. These were all strategies, ways to process (or not process) information, some of which were useful strategies and some of which were not.

MAKING A LEARNING STRATEGY LIBRARY

Remember your first list from the "What works and what doesn't work" activity on page 159. This was the beginning of your learning strategy library.

Copy that list out again into an exercise book, or on to a coloured piece of paper you can stick on the wall above your desk, or into your phone as a note-to-self—anywhere that you can access easily and where you can add to the list when you need to.

If you haven't done the activity, you just need to come up with some ways to learn or study that you have used in the past—strategies that have worked well for you—and write them in here.

Make a table with the strategies in one column, the subjects you might apply them to in the next column, and then a couple more columns where you can tick them off later—after you have tested if they work or not.

Learning strategy library				
Strategy	**Subject**	**Effective**	**Ineffective**	**Why?**
Mindmaps	Biology			
Plastic models	Chemistry			
Role play	History			
Flashcards	Spanish			

Now take a look at some of the sensory-specific learning strategies listed below and pick out any ideas that you would be prepared to try. Add them to your learning strategy library. You might like to choose more from the group that you think is your sensory strength from Chapter 1.

Visual: Use video, film, photographs, mindmaps; use colour in notes; underline or highlight key points; draw pictures, diagrams, graphs.

Auditory: Read out loud; record important school work and play it back; learn from radio programmes or podcasts; teach someone else; have discussions and debates.

Kinesthetic: Use role play, acting out, field trips, experiments, models, flashcards; move around while you read; make mindmaps of key points; study with others; play question-and-answer games.

web links

There are many great websites that are set up to provide you with all the information you need for school subjects—and often in a more visual or interactive way than in the classroom.

http://www.khanacademy.org. This has really clear clips explaining every part of most subjects.

http://www.quizlet.com. This has a flashcard maker for most school subjects.

http://www.bbc.co.uk/gcsebitesize. This gives summary information for most school subjects.

There are other websites that have a collection of great free sites for students all together on one page, for example http://www.taolearn.com/students.php.

MAKING SUMMARY NOTES

In Chapter 1 "Learning to learn" we covered the three sensory styles of learning—seeing, hearing and doing.

Here is a study technique that is **visual** and **auditory** and **kinesthetic**, through which you can learn by:

- looking
- listening and talking, and
- doing.

If you use this study technique, whatever your learning style is, it will be catered for. You will get the information in the way that suits you best, as well as all the other ways.

This requires the use of a graphic organizer for information—one that only focuses on the key points you need and has a built-in system that checks for understanding and completeness. As you saw in Chapter 2 "Essay writing skills", there are many graphic organizers available for note-making and all forms of writing. This is one type that works very well for studying.

TIPS

Remember:

The best students in the world use a variety of study strategies, and they continually modify their study habits to suit their subjects and their school system.

THOrTmaps

This is a single information processing technique that incorporates all three sensory styles of learning covered in Chapter 1, as well as all the ideas on memory and the information on the brain covered in this chapter.

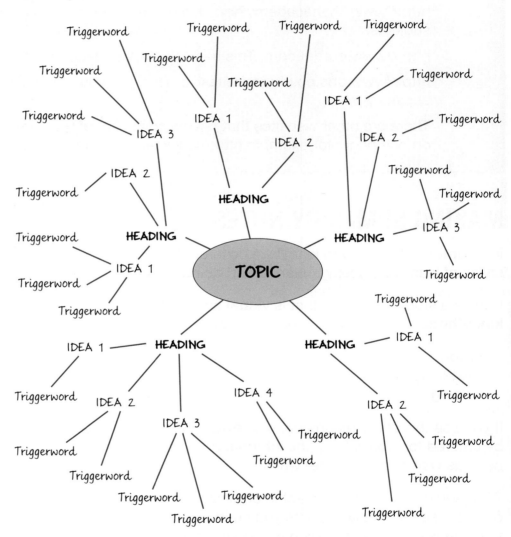

Spider-diagrams, brainstorms, mindmaps might be very familiar but this is a new version of an old idea that will help you to process all the information you have in most of your subjects and understand and remember it well.

There are some subjects for which a THOrTmap is not appropriate. For most of the mathematical subjects such as statistics, calculus, basic maths, arithmetic, etc you would not use a THOrTmap to represent the information you are given. In those subjects there is usually a basic core of information that is best learned by doing many calculations—taking a topic such as "solving simultaneous equations" and doing lots and lots of practice problems until you have got the pattern. Once you have got one pattern, you can move on to the next. There isn't much need for summarizing large quantities of information. Similarly, in learning sports or PE, this kind of information summarizing tool might not be of much use. These THOrTmaps are a study technique purely for all the information-heavy subjects at school such as geography, history, all the sciences (biology, physics and chemistry, or pure science), English, all the languages, economics, business studies, etc.

The made-up word **THOrT**, stands for the four levels of information contained in one THOrTmap.

- **T**opics
- **H**eadings
- Ideas in **Or**der, and
- **T**riggerwords

When you are summarizing a chapter of your textbook or a chunk of your own notes, you simply pick one topic, put that in the middle of the page, add to it all the main headings as your second layer, then the ideas in order as your third layer and lastly the key words—what we call "triggerwords"—because they trigger your memory of all the ideas.

This is a way to make memorable summaries of important school work. When you make a THOrTmap, instead of writing down all your information, you just write the most important points in a special way that helps you remember and join all the key points together with lines. You can use colour, symbols, arrows, whatever you like because a THOrTmap is a representation on paper of the way your mind processes information—the way your brain connects ideas—and so no two THOrTmaps will ever look the same.

Here are some of the important things that make a THOrTmap work.

- There should be no more than five branches at any point—to make every point on the map easier to remember by facilitating movement of chunks of information into long-term memory.
- Each main branch on the map creates a different pattern, which helps retrieval.
- Use key points and details rather than whole paragraphs of information.
- Information is connected from the **big picture** down to the **detail** in the same way as your brain organizes and stores information.
- You can add colour, small pictures and diagrams to the THOrTmap to make it appeal to the right as well as the left side of the brain.

The other thing that makes THOrTmaps work as a study technique is the process you use to build and review them. If you can incorporate all three sensory styles of learning as well as the key review times for best memorization into your process, then you will have a brilliant study technique—one that suits everyone. This whole process is called **Get Working**.

ACTIVITY

ATL skills: thinking, organization

 Time: 30 minutes

  Individual or whole class

MAKING A THORTMAP

For this exercise you are going to need:

- approximately 10 pages of notes—either your own or from a textbook—from one of the information-heavy subjects you study
- a few clean sheets of paper (unlined usually works best).

This is a practice exercise to help you learn how to summarize information and make useful study notes. Go through the process, one step at a time. Complete each step before you move on to the next step.

Get Working: Part 1—making study notes/summarizing technique

Imagine you are studying seven weeks before a test or exam. You are sticking to your timetable, you've got your desk and chair height right, you've got some water and fruit available, you've got some instrumental music playing, and you have in front of you some of your important subject notes that you need to understand and summarize.

Step 1

Skim-read every page. Just pass your eyes over every page that you are intending to summarize, making sure that you look at—not read, just look at—every word, picture and diagram. This is a ***very important stage*** that many people don't do, which can make a huge difference. This stage gives your brain the big picture, the structure of the information, and you will pick up what the main topic is as well as the headings and some keywords. Also, the information contained in the pictures, graphs and diagrams will add to your growing base of knowledge on this topic.

Step 2

Take a clean page, turn it sideways (landscape) and in the centre of the page write the first main **TOPIC** and add to it all the **HEADINGS**, as branches. You should include no more than five headings for one topic. If you have more than five headings you need to start a second or maybe even a third THOrTmap.

Step 3

Now go back to the first page of the notes/textbook. Pick up a highlighter pen and start actively reading the material, searching for the keywords in each sentence and highlighting them. These are **triggerwords**. They will be the most important words in each sentence, the words without which the sentence makes no sense, usually nouns and verbs. Highlight **only one or two triggerwords per sentence**. Make sure you are not highlighting whole sentences, just one or two words per sentence.

Do you remember the visual/auditory/kinesthetic analysis from Chapter 1 "Learning about learning"? This step is the visual part—involving processing information by ***looking***.

Step 4

Now you shift all the highlighted triggerwords to your emerging THOrTmap and group the triggerwords around key **IDEAS**. Attach the triggerwords to the ideas, and attach the ideas in order to the headings as branches. Remember, no more than 5 branches at any point on the THOrTmap.

In Step 4 you are doing something with the information, taking key words and arranging them on the THOrTmap, transforming linear information into graphical information. This is the kinesthetic part — processing information by **doing** something with it.

Step 5

When you have finished your THOrTmap, you will have a page of words that appeals very much to the left side of your brain but has little to attract the right side. Now you need to go back and add in shape, colour, shading, small pictures, diagrams, cartoons to make your THOrTmap more visually appealing and involve the right side of your brain as well as the left.

At this point you can also add links between points and ideas that you may not have seen before or connect two different things with a small picture between them.

Step 6

Lastly, you need to pick up your newly created THOrTmap and talk about all the branches on your THOrTmap, turning them back into sentences, out loud, in your own words. When you can talk your way through any branch of the THOrTmap clearly and easily, you know that you have understood it—you have learned it! If you find you can't talk your way through a particular branch of your THOrTmap and understand it, it just means that you don't have quite enough detail in your THOrTmap. Go back to the relevant notes, pull out a few more triggerwords and add them to your THOrTmap. Now read it out loud to yourself again. Once you can do it, you have got it. You are finished.

This completes the first cycle on the diagram below: the **Look—Do—Listen** stage.

Notice how this part of the study system uses all your senses—seeing, doing and hearing. So no matter what your learning style you will be able to process the information in the way that suits you best, and also in the other ways as well. This will help you to learn in the way you prefer and also to become a more flexible learner.

TIPS

Remember that if you keep the right side of your brain involved you will remember twice as much.

TIPS

This is the auditory part—processing information by talking and **listening**.

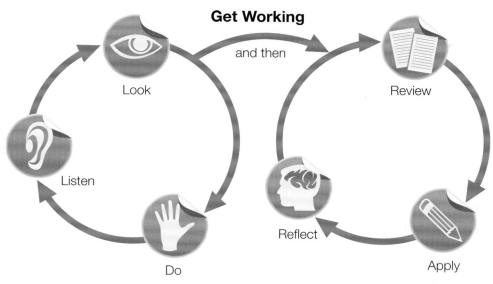

Use all your senses to remember what you learn

Get Working

Look
and then
Review
Listen
Do
Reflect
Apply

Once that is all complete, you can move to the second phase of the Get Working process, which is the **Review—Apply—Reflect** cycle.

Get Working: Part 2—shifting into long-term working memory

In Chapter 1 "Learning about learning" you were introduced to the importance of review in remembering important subject information. Once you have made your THOrTmaps, you need to make sure you can remember them by building into your study regime a cycle of regular review.

Step 7

Once you have finished making your THOrTmap, you need to take a break. Get up, move around, go and have something to drink. Come back in 10 minutes.

After 10 minutes, pick up your completed THOrTmap and read through it again, then turn it face down and draw it again on a clean sheet of paper—as a draft copy only. Don't worry about reproducing any pictures or colours or shading, just use those things in your memory to help recall the information that is on the map. When you finish, check back with the original and notice what you don't yet know. Highlight that part on the original so you will remember to focus particularly on that part in your next review. This is your **10-minute review**.

Step 8

In one day's time you need to read through the same THOrTmap again, then turn it face down like you have just done and recreate it on a blank page. This will be your **1-day review**.

Step 9

In one week's time you need to repeat the review process again. This will be your **1-week review**.

Step 10

If you are studying more than four weeks before an exam you would also build in one more review after four weeks. This then becomes your **1-month review**.

Step 11

Once you know your stuff, the next thing you need to practise is how to answer real exam questions. This requires you to be able to get hold of old exam papers, extract relevant questions and answer them in the right time frame, without referring to your notes. In some countries you can find old exam questions online. If you are unable to do this, then ask your teachers to provide exam-level questions for you to practise on. This is the **Apply Step**.

Step 12

Did this study technique work for you? Did any parts work especially well? Write up your results in your learning strategy library. Remember that it is only one technique and you need to mix and match different techniques to find what suits you best. This is the **Reflect Step**.

ATL skills: reflection

METACOGNITION

Always notice and be willing to experiment with study parameters.

- Where do you study best?
- When?
- How?
- With whom?
- Using which resources?
- Which strategies work for which subjects?

Do more of anything that helps you study, remember and understand better.

Do less of what doesn't help.

In the exam room

Once you get into the exam room you need all your faculties to be functioning at the maximum level, as well as good exam-room technique.

Nerves first—some people get very nervous when faced with a major exam, to the point where their nerves get in the way of them putting in their best performance.

In an exam, have you ever felt confident, relaxed and focused, as though you are concentrating and remembering well?

You might have felt like that when you learned to count or read, when you learned to ride a bike or skate, when you scored a try or shot a basket or whatever.

Imagine how good it would feel if you stood up in front of the whole school to speak or sing and they all stood up and cheered and shouted—just imagine it! Or imagine what it would be like if you scored the winning goal or the winning try for your favourite team. Imagine how great you would feel.

In the activity on the next page, you will be establishing a connection between the part of your brain that generates feelings and the part responsible for a unique physical action. If you connect motion and emotion you create a full kinesthetic linkage.

ACTIVITY

ATL skills: reflection, thinking

 Time: 15 minutes

  Individual or whole class

HOW WOULD YOU MOST LIKE TO FEEL IN AN EXAM OR TEST?

There is a way of establishing a connection between the part of your brain that generates feelings and the part responsible for a unique physical action. If you connect motion and emotion you create a full kinesthetic linkage.

For individuals: To do this activity you need to be able to visualize. This means it is going to be hard to read what to do and to do the exercise at the same time. Read through the whole of the exercise so you know what to do, then get someone else to talk you through the visualization the first time—with them reading the script out loud.

For a whole class: Your teacher will need to read the visualization script while students close their eyes and imagine.

To do this activity you will have to remember or imagine a time when you were feeling confident. You need to bring up a memory of feeling confident from your own life, for example, when you first learned to ride a bike or skate or swim. Do you remember how confident you felt then? Or you can use your imagination to create an imaginary time when you are feeling confident, for example, you could imagine that you are the lead in the school production and are getting applause from all the audience for a brilliant performance, or maybe you could imagine playing football for your country and scoring the winning goal at the World Cup. It doesn't matter at all if it is a real memory or an imagined memory—your mind makes no distinction between the two.

When you have thought of something to use, you are ready to go through the visualization. The visualization will help you to generate a feeling of confidence inside yourself and then to link that feeling to a physical action. The physical action that you could use is a clenched fist, in a grab action pulled back towards yourself, as you might do if you were celebrating a great success.

This is like a symbol of success anyway. So when you get the feeling of confidence coming up inside you during the visualization, you are going to capture it in a clenched fist. That's all—very simple.

When you have done this exercise once with someone else reading the visualization script you will be able to do it yourself, at home. If you try this exercise once a day for about three weeks you will find that a strong link has been made in your brain between the physical action and the feeling. Then anytime you need to feel confident, all you will have to do is clench your fist in the same way and you will regenerate that same feeling of confidence straight away. And because you can't feel anxious or nervous at the same time as feeling confident, your nervousness will disappear and you will be able to concentrate well and perform to your best in any exam.

So, set up someone to read through the script printed here and all you have to do is relax, maybe put your head down on your desk, close your eyes and be still.

Visualization script

This needs to be read quietly, in a calm voice, pausing when you see the "...".

First, I just want you to relax.

Breathe deeply and relax your back, relax your neck, just relax.

Now what I want you to do first is to imagine a big blank TV screen in your mind, not switched on yet, nothing on the screen right now ...

Now turn the TV on and the first picture that comes up on the screen is you, in that moment when you are feeling confident, feeling great—and remember it can be from your own past or from your imagination. See yourself now on the TV screen in that moment, feeling confident and just pause that image for a moment, freeze the image on the screen ... and notice where you are when you are feeling so confident ... are you inside or outside? ... are there other people there or are you on your own? ... fill in the background on the screen and the foreground ... and now notice the colours that are present on the screen ... now take your colour control and brighten up all the colours, notice them really bright and clear ... and now you can bring up the sound too and notice what you can hear when you are feeling so confident ... and now notice what you are saying to yourself when you are feeling so confident ... and now I want you to move, I want you to move closer to the screen and notice how the picture is getting bigger ... and closer to the screen and the picture is getting bigger still until you can step right into that picture and be there, now ... and now release the freeze frame and go through that moment of feeling confident and notice how it feels to feel confident

... and when that great feeling of confidence comes up inside you I want you to take one of your hands and clench it tight into a fist and lock in that feeling ... lock in that wonderful feeling of confidence with a clenched fist ... [long pause] ... and then just relax that hand again, stretch out those fingers again, let it go and open your eyes and come back to this room and stretch and welcome back!

That exercise showed you what to do and how to do it. If you want it to work for you when you need it, you will have to practise that same visualization once a day for about three weeks to make the brain connections strong.

You can do this at home yourself now. You just need to:

1. remember or imagine feeling confident—go through what can you see and hear and how it feels
2. when you notice the feeling, lock it in with a clenched fist
3. practise once a day for about 21 days.

Then, when you need to feel confident, you just clench your fist, in the same way.

Once you have established the connection in your brain and created the trigger, when you need to feel confident, sitting in that exam room, all you have to do is fire off your trigger—clench that fist and you will recreate that confident feeling throughout your body, your nervousness will disappear and you will be able to apply the whole of your brain to your task, concentrating and remembering well.

EXAM/TEST-TAKING TECHNIQUES

When you are in the exam or test situation, you need to use good answer-writing techniques. They can make a tremendous difference, so remember these tips when you are in the test room with your paper in front of you.

1. Skim-read the whole paper and highlight the instructions. For example:

   do all of Section A
   and 3 out of 6 in Section B
   then 5 out of 7 in Section C

   This should keep you from making simple mistakes and also give your unconscious mind time to draw together the necessary material for later questions while you are answering the first.

2. Allocate your time. If your exam lasts 2 hours and is marked out of 100 marks that means:

   - 120 minutes for 100 marks
   - 1.2 minutes per mark.

   So a 5-mark question should take 6 minutes, a 10-mark question should take 12 minutes, etc.

   Write in the time you should spend on each question and, most importantly, stick to time.

   There will be some questions that you can complete in less than the allocated time, which will give you a few extra minutes at the end of the paper for rechecking.

3. Always start with the easiest questions—to get your thinking going and your confidence up.

4. Read each question carefully and highlight the verb—what the examiner wants. For example, there is a great deal of difference between the following command terms.

   a. **List**: Give a sequence of brief answers with no explanation.

   b. **Compare**: Give and account of the similarities between two (or more) items or situations, referring to both (all) of them throughout.

   c. **Discuss**: Offer a considered and balanced review that includes a range of arguments, factors or hypothesis. Opinions or conclusions should be presented clearly and supported by appropriate evidence

   d. **Describe**: Give a detailed account or picture of a situation, event, pattern or process.

5. If you are able to, leave a generous space in your answer book after each answer—this makes your paper easier to mark and gives you room to add in extra information at the end if necessary.

6. Use graphic organizers (such as THOrTmaps) as planners for long answers, and include them in your answer book—examiners may give you marks for showing your planning for an essay answer as well as the answer itself.

7. If you run out of time (which you won't do if you stick to time):

   - for calculation-type exams—explain what you would have done to solve the problem without actually doing it (in calculation exams often more than half the marks are for the process, less than half for getting the right answer)
   - for written-type exams—show the outline of your answer as a list of key points or a graphic organizer, but don't write the essay.

If you have spare time at the end of the exam when you think you have finished, never leave early—even if you are allowed to. Stay and relax. Once you have relaxed you might remember new things you could add to your answers, and you can go back and add to them in the spaces left. Don't change any answers unless you are absolutely, one hundred per cent sure you got it wrong the first time—first thoughts are usually right.

KEY POINTS OF THE CHAPTER

ATL skills

- Organization
- Thinking
- Information literacy
- Communication
- Reflection
- Self-management

The key stages in learning to study for tests, exams, projects and assignments

1. Self-motivation
2. Timetabling
3. Making good notes in class
4. Organizing your study environment at home
5. Noticing how you study best and being prepared to try different strategies
6. Making good summaries of key information
7. Overcoming nerves
8. Practising good techniques in the test environment

Useful websites

http://www.bbc.co.uk/gcsebitesize

http://www.freeology.com

http://www.johndclare.net and http://www.spartacus.schoolnet.co.uk. These are good sites for history, all countries, all ages.

http://www.khanacademy.org. This provides really clear YouTube clips explaining every part of most subjects.

http://www.mrbartonmaths.com/goodsites.htm. Provides free maths sites for IGCSE.

http://www.quizlet.com and http://www.easynotecards.com/index. Here you will find flashcard makers for most subjects.

http://www.s-cool.co.uk and http://www.bbc.co.uk/schools/gcsebitesize/. Both are good resources for all subjects for IGCSE.

http://www.swipestudy.com. Provides self-tests in most subjects— sent to your phone!

http://www.taolearn.com/students.php. This provides a reference list of the best free sites to help your study.

http://www.youtube.com/watch?v=rSwnODMNULI

http://www.youtube.com/watch?v=QqjcCvzWwww&feature=related

http://www.youtube.com/watch?v=ZZ6g70BXbW8&feature=related

CHAPTER 7

OBJECTIVES

In this chapter we will be:

- looking further at how you learn and how you interpret the world
- reviewing what we have learned from earlier chapters and activities about your learning style
- reflecting on ways in which you can improve as a learner.

You will also be given activities that suit different ways of learning. These will help you think about how you decide which learning strategies suit a particular task.

Let us start by thinking about what we mean by reflection. Below are some definitions from key thinkers in this area that may be helpful.

"A reflection in a mirror is an exact replica of what is in front of it. Reflection in ... practice, however, gives back not what it is, but what might be, an improvement on the original."   Biggs

"You don't learn from experience, you learn from processing your experience." John Dewey

"Reflection deepens learning. The act of reflecting is one which causes us to make sense of what we've learned, why we learned it, and how that particular increment of learning took place. Moreover, reflection is about linking one increment of learning to the wider perspective of learning—heading towards seeing the bigger picture. Reflection is equally useful when our learning has been unsuccessful—in such cases, indeed, reflection can often give us insights into what may have gone wrong with our learning, and how on a future occasion we might avoid now-known pitfalls."   Phil Race

"Learning to learn, or the development of learning power, is getting better at knowing when, how and what to do when you don't know what to do."   Guy Claxton

"Reflection is a way of maximizing learning and minimizing surface approaches.... Reflection also aids deep learning by promoting independent thought"   Karen Hinett

In other words, reflection is a transformational process that goes beyond just thinking about who we are, what mistakes we have made and how what we have learned fits into our wider knowledge about something. Reflection involves thinking about how we can improve ourselves and our learning. As you reflect on what you have learned in this chapter, keep focusing on how you can use that knowledge and insight into your own learning to help you improve and make better choices about the learning strategies and skills you use for different tasks.

REFLECTION

There are two main ways you can use reflection in the MYP, both of which will help make you a better learner:

- as a specific requirement for some subjects
  In the arts, technology and in your personal project there will be a reflective journaling element (which your teacher will explain to you) that is an important part of gaining the specific knowledge you need in that subject.
- as a part of ATL
  Helping you to focus on how you are learning as well as what is, and what is not, working for you. This is what we will focus on here.

Within ATL there are at least three ways you can use reflection to help improve your learning ability and your learning success.

1. Recognizing what you don't yet understand (in any subject) and formulating good questions to ask your teacher.
2. Recognizing your progress in mastering all the ATL skills and thinking about how you can improve.
3. Recognizing the learning strategies and techniques you are using to study and learn and thinking about how effective they are and what you could improve on.

If practiced regularly, reflection in all these three areas will definitely help you to improve your ability to learn and, as a consequence, learning will be easier for you and you will achieve better results.

Reflection on understanding

A key strategy mentioned in the memory section of Chapter 1 was the need, **each night**, for you to **read over all the notes you took at school that day**. This review process will help you move information into long term memory and is an essential part of retaining critical information. When you are engaged in this process you will also notice anything that you wrote down that day that you don't yet understand and you will be able to formulate a suitable question to ask your teacher the next day.

Some good ways to structure questions for your teachers.

- What I understand is .... but what I don't understand is ....
- What I know about this so far is .... but how do I ....?
- Where I am up to in meeting my goal is .... but what do I have to do to ....?
- What I need to know is ....
- The thing I still don't understand is ....
- What do you mean when you say ....?

REVIEW AND REFLECTION ON THE ATL SKILLS

During your studies you should reflect on your learning during the process **and** once you have completed a task. Let's look back at what we have learned about how the ATL skills can help you with your learning. In Chapter 1, "Learning about learning", you were introduced to the seven ATL skills and given some reflection questions. Now that you have read the book, tried out some of the tasks and thought about the skills, it is time to reflect on what you have learned and also to think about your overall strengths and areas for improvement in each of the skill areas. Hopefully you have learned about and experimented with a range of strategies and approaches, some familiar and some new, which you can use to increase your bank of skills and help you approach tasks in new and different ways.

To help you in your reflection, let's first take a quick look back at what was covered in each chapter in terms of the ATL skills.

Chapter	Key ideas and skills covered
Chapter 1: Learning about learning *Reflecting on and understanding your own learning preferences can help you to develop and expand your abilities in other learning styles and approaches in order to adopt a multi-sensory learning style and become a more flexible learner.* *Looking at memory and how you can improve your long-term memory.* *Developing your skills in collaborative learning.*	• Different learning strategies and skills to improve your learning • How you can discover your own learning style • **Metacognitive skills** related to thinking about how you plan, monitor and assess your learning • **Cognitive skills** related to how you process information, use your memory and develop study habits • **Affective skills** related to your mood, motivation and attitude • How you learn in terms of your preferred sensory style(s) (V, A, K) • Your preferred study environment • The importance of shifting information from your short- to your long-term memory in each sensory system • How the memory works, chunking information and the importance of review • How to improve memory techniques using your imagination • The benefits of collaborative learning and tools to help you with this
Chapter 2: Essay writing skills *Carefully managing your time and working with others through the stages involved in organizing, planning, writing and reviewing different types of essays.* *Understanding, developing and adapting the specific skills and structural and linguistic features of different essay types.* *Maintaining academic honesty.*	• The importance of **managing your time** at each stage of the writing process • Using your **information literacy skills** to access, select, **organize** and **reference** information as you work through the stages of writing an essay • The importance of **thinking skills** required to generate ideas, plan and organize your arguments and ideas on paper • The role of **communication skills** in structuring and expressing your own ideas clearly on paper and examining how other writers communicate their messages
Chapter 3: Using the design cycle *Working through the stages of the cycle from investigation—which identifies a range of relevant primary and secondary sources—to planning and creating a product before producing thoughtful and balanced evaluations.* *Managing your time efficiently.* *Maintaining academic honesty.*	• The importance of **collaboration** when working in a group • **Information literacy** when checking the reliability of websites and referencing your sources • The importance of **thinking skills** in planning and approaching a task in different ways and thinking **critically and creatively** about a problem • The important role of **reflection** throughout the process and of evaluation at the end, to see where you succeeded and outline areas for improvement

Chapter	Key ideas and skills covered
Chapter 4: Scientific method *Working alone or collaboratively, following the key stages of scientific method: generating viable questions and hypotheses, researching material, analysing data, drawing thoughtful conclusions and communicating your results.* *Reflecting on each stage of the process.* *Producing accurate, reliable and verifiable experiments.*	• Using **thinking skills** to create a question that generates measureable qualitative and/or quantitative data • Using appropriate **research** and **reflection skills** when developing and testing an hypothesis • Analysing data • Drawing conclusions about your hypothesis • Using **communication skills** when reporting your findings • The importance of **organization skills** in managing your time, the materials and the process • The key role of **collaboration skills** in working with others
Chapter 5: Presentation skills *Working through the stages involved in planning, preparing, practising and giving presentations, either alone or collaboratively.* *Developing the strategies and communication and information literacy skills needed to deliver informative and engaging presentations.*	• Different ways of presenting, using computer presentation tools that organize information sequentially for an audience or in terms of big picture and details • **Thinking** about the content and **organization** of your material to suit a particular audience • **Communication skills**—techniques and methods to help make delivery of information both engaging and entertaining for an audience • The importance of developing **collaborative skills** when working on group presentations
Chapter 6: Assessments, tests and exams *Outlining the key steps in learning to study for tests, exams, projects and assignments: motivating yourself, timetabling a schedule, organizing your study environment, and improving your note-taking and summary skills.* *By recognizing and developing your range of learning strategies, you will learn to overcome nerves and apply these techniques to perform successfully in assessments when under pressure.*	• The importance of being active in your learning • How your outlook shapes your motivation • The need to be able to access a range of **thinking** and learning strategies • The role of **organization skills** in planning and managing your time • How to look after the brain • How to **organize** your study space • How to avoid procrastination and generate motivation to perform well in assessments • Study tips for preparing for and taking exams and tests

Below are a series of ATL reflection questions that build on those in Chapter 1 in the context of what you have learned in each chapter. Use the reflection questions as a guide to help you identify areas where you are confident and areas that require further work. You may be able to add further questions of your own as part of your reflection.

ATL skills	I am very good at this	I am ok at this	I need to work on this
Communication • How well do I prioritize, organize and present my ideas in speech, writing or through visual means? • How able am I to adapt my language, tone and register to suit my audience and purpose? • How well do I use and interpret a range of content-specific terminology? • How well do I use reading strategies to gather information before, during and after reading? • How well do I use a range of media to access, organize and synthesize information and ideas? • How well do I use a range of media when communicating my ideas to others in verbal, visual and written forms?			
Evidence of my ability or need to improve			
Collaboration • How well do I work with others? • How able am I to accept others' opinions and respect their points of view? • How willing am I to put aside my prejudices and biases when working in groups? • How confident am I taking a leading role when working in groups? • How well do I work as a team player, listening to instructions, accepting roles I am given and making suggestions to help solve a problem? • How good a listener am I? How well do I focus on other people's ideas without allowing my own to interfere with my thinking? • How good am I at critically analysing and using others people's ideas?			
Evidence of my ability or need to improve			

ATL skills	I am very good at this	I am ok at this	I need to work on this
Information literacy • How comfortable am I communicating my ideas using technologies for presentations, journals, essays and projects? • How adept am I at accessing, sorting and evaluating information from a range of sources? • How good am I at identifying and using different (primary and secondary) sources? • How good am I at assessing the accuracy and reliability of information? • How good am I at critically analysing information (detecting bias) and making connections? • How good am I at referencing my sources and acknowledging other people's ideas?			

Evidence of my ability or need to improve

Organization—managing time, others and task • How well do I use graphic organizers, concept maps, THorT charts in planning different activities and making notes? • How good am I at breaking down my tasks into smaller steps? • How effective am I at setting myself short- and long-term goals and deadlines and sticking to them? • How good am I at prioritizing information and ideas in my work? • How good am I at prioritizing tasks? • How good am I at balancing my time between work, relaxation and other commitments? • How effective am I at monitoring and evaluating the way in which I approach different tasks? • How good am I at organizing my learning materials?			

Evidence of my ability or need to improve

ATL skills	I am very good at this	I am ok at this	I need to work on this
Reflection • How good am I at identifying my own strengths and limitations and thinking of ways that I can improve and develop as a learner? • How good am I at seeking feedback and understanding how to improve? • How good am I at measuring my progress by reflecting at different stages in the learning process? • How good am I at reflecting with others as part of a group? • How well do I use different strategies and methods of reflection (journals, portfolios, etc)? • How often do I review the effectiveness of my reflections in helping me learn? • How well do I review the effectiveness of my reflections in helping me learn?			

Evidence of my ability or need to improve

Thinking • How well do I reflect on my thinking as a process? • Am I good at evaluating the strategies I adopt for a task and/or to solve a problem? • How good am I at posing questions to stimulate my own and others' thinking on a topic or problem? • How well do I plan and brainstorm for different tasks? • How good am I at analysing problems from a range of perspectives? • How well do I use the inquiry cycle? • How good am I at applying my knowledge and skills creatively to solve problems?			

Evidence of my ability or need to improve

ATL skills	I am very good at this	I am ok at this	I need to work on this
Transfer • How good am I at seeing and understanding the central ideas within each subject and at making connections with the central ideas in other subject areas? • How good am I at transferring my skills between one subject and another or one task and another? • How good am I at using my knowledge and understanding from one subject to help me in another?			

Evidence of my ability or need to improve

Now use your reflection to highlight ways to improve yourself as a learner. You could use the chart below to complete your ideas

My strengths	Areas for improvement	Strategies to improve

REFLECTION ON HOW YOU LEARN BEST—METACOGNITION

Metacognition simply means recognizing the learning strategies and techniques you are using to study and learn each subject and thinking about how effective they are and what you could improve on. This is something that needs to be done on an on-going basis, through reflection each night, and simply requires you to answer **four** questions—**one** at the beginning, and **three** at the end of your homework/study.

Before you start

1. What am I planning on studying/learning tonight?
    (What subjects, what tasks, what goals?)

At the end

2. How did I approach my studying/learning?
    (What were you actually doing? Reading, highlighting key points, making written summaries, drawing diagrams or flowcharts, watching videos, making flashcards, listening to podcasts, using a particular website?)
3   How well did it work?
    (Did you learn your topic well, did your techniques work, do you now understand and remember what you wanted to, have you achieved the goal(s) you set yourself?)
4. What could I have done differently?
    (What would be another way you could approach that same task—another study method, another technique, strategy or website that you might use next time you have a similar task?)

Reflecting on reflection

If you follow this system you will end up with:

*   reflections on what you are learning and what you haven't yet understood
*   reflections on your learning skill competency and what skills you need to work on
*   reflections on how you are learning and what techniques work best for you.

All of these points will help make you into a brilliant learner who can handle any academic challenge.

WHAT MAKES YOU UNIQUE AS A LEARNER?

Now you have thought about your own strengths and limitations in each of the ATL skills areas and how you learn best, let's look in more detail at the following questions.

- **How do I know?** This is the way I perceive the world and acquire knowledge:

  a practical focus on facts, processes, details

  or

  an imaginative intuitive focus on meanings, possibilities and concepts.

- **How do I think?** This is the way I form and process ideas:

  ordering ideas in a logical linear sequential way from part to whole, verbalizing ideas and focusing on the world around me

  or

  ordering ideas in random clusters from whole to part, using intuition and private reflection focusing on the inner world.

- **How do I decide?** This is based on my emotional responses and values:

  making rational objective decisions based on logic and rules aiming to please others

  or

  making subjective decisions based on considerations of self and others.

- **How do I act?** This is the way I approach a task and how I work with others or alone:

  approaching tasks in a systematic sequential manner, following schedules and working with others

  or

  approaching tasks in a random fashion, adapting to changes and working alone.

The way we learn and interpret the world around us varies greatly from one individual to another. In Chapter 1, "Learning about learning", you already considered your sensory learning style, how you prefer to process information through your senses and how this affects your ability to learn in different environments. You also read about the importance of affective, cognitive and metacognitive skills in developing your range of learning skills, strategies and approaches. However, to help you develop your reflection on how you learn and make sense of the world as an individual, consider some specific examples of these behaviours and think about other aspects that can affect how you learn and how you make sense of the world around you. Look at the following examples and reflect on how they may apply to you as an individual.

The way you perceive and interpret the world

Sight

Sight is one of the primary senses we use when trying to process information and make sense of the world. However, it is worth asking: Do we all see things in the same way? For example, when we look at an image such as the one here, we may see different things—you may see the vase or the profiles of two faces.

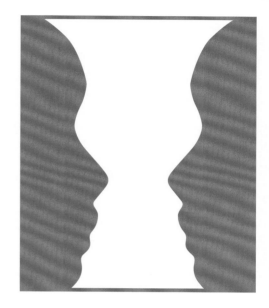

Consider the following points.

- How do short-sighted, long-sighted, colour-blind people see and interpret the world differently from someone with perfect sight?
- How do people with conditions such as autism see the world differently? Look at this video of Daniel Tammet whose linguistic, numerical and visual synaesthesia means he sees the world very differently from most people: http://www.ted.com/talks/daniel_tammet_different_ways_of_knowing.html.
- How do your expectations about what you are going to see affect what you see or what you fail to see?
- How often do we fail to see certain obvious things when we are focusing on something else. Look at this classic example: http://www.youtube.com/watch?v=IGQmdoK_ZfY&feature=related.

Hearing

Think of a time when you heard the teacher give instructions to the whole class and you did something differently from one of your classmates.

Even among similar cultures there are differences in the way we learn and interpret things and make meanings using **language**. Consider some of the following differences between the United States and the UK.

- A "stroller" in the USA is a pushchair, while in the UK it is someone who takes a leisurely walk.
- A "flat" in the UK is somewhere you live, but in the USA it is a punctured tire (spelled "tyre" in the UK!).

Language is also full of ambiguity. How would you interpret a sign that read "Fine for parking here"? Is it legal to park here, or if you park here will you be fined? Think about how different people might interpret this depending on their familiarity with the English language.

Think also of the confusion caused by commands phrased as questions, offers or statements as in the example below.

Command	Make me a cup of tea.	Get out!
Question	Are you making tea?	Are you still here?
Offer	Shall I put the kettle on for you?	Would you like me to get the door for you?
Statement	It's time for a cup of tea.	I thought everyone had left.

Since our language is constantly evolving the meanings of words change. Consider the impact of technological change on words that may mean different things to people of different ages. Consider, for example the world of computers:

- mouse
- bytes
- monitor
- memory
- firewall
- phishing

Cultural background, upbringing and experiences

These too have an enormous influence on the way we learn and how we interpret the world around us.

Everyday objects have a different significance for different people, depending on our culture. Even within cultures they can carry different significances on different occasions.

- Tattoo—rebellion, tribal marking, fashion statement
- Sarong—souvenir, traditional dress, fashion accessory
- Flip-flops—fashion accessory, relaxation, vacation
- Candle—symbol of hope, memorial, emergency light source, religious symbol
- Horse—food, wild animal, companion, workforce, competitor
- Dog—companion, guide (worker), food, security
- Flowers—funeral, love, decoration

Different aspects of our environments carry different symbolic meanings within different cultures.

- Seasons in some cultures are associated with concepts and cycles such as life, death, rebirth and change but other cultures have different seasons. Do they make the same comparisons?

- Colours have different significances and connotations in different cultures. White, for example, in Western cultures symbolizes innocence and purity, submission and cowardice, as well as having religious connotations, while in some Asian cultures it is associated with mourning and death.

The way common sounds are described differs enormously between cultures. Look at how different countries describe the noise a cockerel or rooster makes.

- In Dutch it is kukeleku.
- In English it is cock-a-doodle-do.
- In French it is cocorico.
- In Russian it is kukareku.
- In Japanese it is ko-ke-kok-ko-o.
- In Urdu it is kuklooku.
- In Spanish it is kikiriki.

http://www.eleceng.adelaide.edu.au/personal/dabbott/animal.html

Experience of learning

Depending on your cultural upbringing, your experience of school can vary dramatically. For example, you may have been brought up to regard the teacher as an authority figure and source of all knowledge or as someone who facilitates the process of learning and discovery. You may have been taught that learning is focused on memorizing facts and information. You may have been conditioned to work independently and see yourself as competing against other students in your class or you may see learning as a cooperative activity that you all do together.

Your personality and attitudes

- Are you an optimist or a pessimist? Do you see the glass as half-full or half-empty?

- What suggestions does the word **flight** have for you?

- Are you an introvert or an extrovert?

- Do you prefer to try things out or think things through?

- Do you prefer working in groups or on your own?

Stress

Do you suffer from stress? Many students let their emotions interfere with clear thinking. The stress they feel prevents them from thinking logically and clearly about a situation. Thoughts such as, "I will never be able to finish my work" or "I can't see myself ever passing this test", prevent them thinking clearly about the reality of their situation—exactly how many tasks they have to complete and what exactly they need to do in order to study for and pass the test. The key is training your mind to think rationally and focus on the details of the task in hand. Look back at Chapter 7, "Assessments, tests and exams" and review some of the strategies that helped you deal with stress.

Your motivation

Motivation is a key factor in your success. It is what drives all your efforts. And there are two main types of motivation:

- intrinsic or self-motivation—motivation that comes from within you
- extrinsic motivation—motivation that comes from external factors such as pleasing your parents, or the rewards success will bring you.

Relying on others to motivate you can be a problem when dealing with your school work, so it is important to create strategies that promote intrinsic or self-motivation, motivation that comes from within you.

web links

To find out more about your motivation for learning try taking this test.
http://agelesslearner.com/assess/motivationstyle.html

In Chapter 7 we looked at how your attitude and perspective towards tests, assessments and exams shape your motivation, and we considered a number of strategies to increase your motivation. You explored factors that helped you learn well and others that hindered your success as a learner.

Another good strategy is to look at other people who have been successful in their field. Consider this group of people below.

- Bill Gates—founder of Microsoft
- Aung San Suu Kyi—leader of Burmese opposition

- Walt Disney—a pioneer in film-making and animation, and founder of Walt Disney Film Studios
- Richard Branson—billionaire businessman and owner of Virgin companies
- Wangari Muta Maathai—Kenyan environmental and political activist
- Ellen Johnson Sirleaf—President and Head of Government of Liberia
- Henry Ford—billionaire founder of Ford motor company
- JK Rowling—bestselling author of Harry Potter series and first billionaire author
- Amelia Earhart—US aviation pioneer and author
- Albert Einstein—the father of modern physics who developed the theory of general relativity
- Agatha Christie—famous detective novelist

All successful people, right? But another factor you may not know, which connects them all, is that they all suffered failure and struggled in various aspects of their life, before achieving their successes. And very often this is the case with very successful people. What makes them different from others who fail and continue failing is their attitude to failure. How you view your failures is as important as how you view your successes. As Henry Ford, the car manufacturer said:

> *"Failure is the opportunity to begin again more intelligently."*

Many people with dyslexia and other learning difficulties have struggled in school but a surprisingly large number have become hugely successful in later life. If we try to analyse why, it may be due to the fact that having struggled or been told their way of doing something did not work, they persevered and adapted and found an alternative method that worked for them. They never lost their self-belief and their conviction that they could succeed, despite others telling them they were wrong. Their reaction to setbacks was to persevere and find alternative ways to overcome challenges or obstacles to success. These qualities, and this sort of approach to challenges, are key to success.

Think about role models in your school—current pupils or some who have left. What qualities and behaviours helped them succeed at school and beyond?

CASE STUDY

Carol Dweck—Fixed Mindset vs Growth Mindset

One role model who inspired psychologist Carol Dweck to begin her research on what leads some people to give up when confronted with failure, while others see failure as a chance to learn from mistakes and improve, was Bruce Jenner, a top Olympic athlete who suffered from a learning disability. Jenner realized that his sporting success was due to his realization of the importance of effort when struggling with his schoolwork. Once he applied the same effort to his sport he made history. Jenner's belief that he could improve through effort was the key to his success.

Carol Dweck's research has revealed that students do better if they think of their intelligence as malleable and flexible rather than fixed and frozen. She found that students with a "fixed mindset", who focus on performance, place high value on success and think intelligence is fixed from birth, are so preoccupied with looking clever that they are often not concerned with learning. They avoid challenges that threaten their self-image, only doing activities at which they will succeed. They often give up easily when encountering obstacles and see effort as pointless or as a sign of low intelligence—something needed only by those lacking ability. Students with a "fixed mindset" make comments like, "I'm no good at maths and physics" or "I am".

In contrast, students with learning goals, or what Dweck calls a "growth mindset", about intelligence believe that the brain is like a muscle than can be strengthened with training as they use it to learn. They are motivated to learn and are more likely to embrace challenges, or take risks, persist in the face of setbacks, learn from criticism and feedback and see failure or mistakes as an opportunity to learn and improve. They regard effort as the key to success and find lessons and inspiration in the success of others.

In one study of adolescents, Dweck, Blackwell and colleagues made students participate in study skills sessions on the brain; in addition, the control group of half the students was given a session on memory while the other half was given training on the growth mindset and how, with training, the brain can improve intelligence and how they could apply this to their studies. Three times as many students in the growth mindset group demonstrated increased effort and engagement compared with the control group. Following their training, the control group's grades continued to decline, while the growth-mindset group showed a clear improvement.

In another study in 2006 focusing on beliefs about intelligence and how they influence learning and academic success, Dweck and her colleagues tested two groups of Columbia University undergraduates, one with a "fixed mindset" and the other with a "growth mindset", and monitored brain activity when giving the students feedback on a test they had taken. They found that in the group with a '"fixed mindset" their brain activity decreased when they were given feedback on how to improve their scores, viewing this as negative feedback and a threat to their beliefs about their own intelligence. In contrast those with a "growth mindset" showed increased brain activity when receiving feedback on the test and on how to improve. While both groups scored similarly on the initial test, on the retest the "growth mindset" group scored significantly higher, correcting many more errors than the "fixed mindset" group.

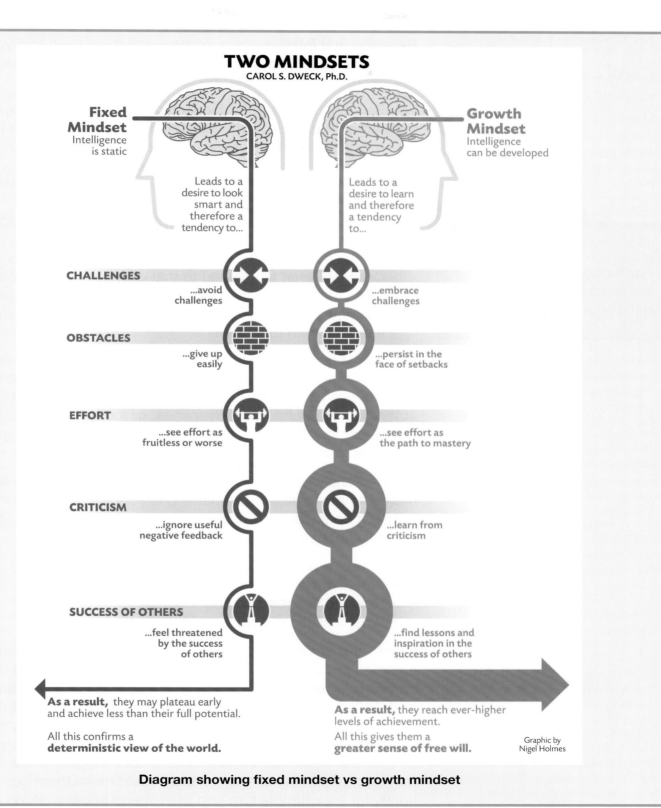

Diagram showing fixed mindset vs growth mindset

So how can you use this information to help you develop as a learner?

Believing that intelligence is innate, something fixed that you are born with, means you can do nothing to improve. Believing effort is the key to improving gives you control.

- Be wary of praise that focuses on your intelligence or ability rather than your effort. Such praise can help create a fixed mindset. Focus on praise and feedback that specifically tells you where you did well and how you can improve.
- Avoid opting for easy challenges and try tasks that extend your abilities.
- See mistakes and failures as opportunities to learn, adapt and improve.
- Think about areas where you once struggled but now do well. Consider what factors led to that change in performance.
- Think of times when you have seen people learn to do things you never thought they would be able to. Consider what factors enabled them to achieve.

web links

For further help go to the website http://www.mindsetworks.com.

For many students anxiety and the fear of failure is a key factor that can affect their motivation. It can cause students to panic when they have to give a presentation in front of the class. It is what causes actors to freeze and forget their lines, or footballers to panic and miss a penalty. But if you can see failure as an opportunity it will help you avoid making the same mistakes again.

Detailed analysis of your failure will help you improve, so take a moment now to analyse something in your life that you consider a failure. It could be in a school context or outside school. Think carefully about it and answer the following questions.

- What went wrong?
- What factors caused it to go wrong?
- How did you react to your failure?
- What lessons did you learn from the experience?

In activities where the smallest of margins makes a difference this is a particularly important skill. In sports such as swimming or sprinting, where the margins between success or failure are as small as 1/1000th of a second, athletes need to look very carefully at where they can pick up these fractions of a second. They may watch tapes of their performance over and over and analyse elements such as their starts, or their tumble turns or their lunges for the line. They may decide that increased flexibility could make them curl more tightly for their tumble turn and then spend hours working on improving their flexibility through a range of exercises. The same is true for you as a learner. Paying attention to the details and working hard to get them right is what will help you turn failure into success.

As we said at the start of this chapter, the key to reflecting on your learning and developing is to **change** and **adapt** the way you approach tasks.

Your intelligence

What does it mean to be intelligent? How do you measure and judge your own intelligence? This is a difficult question and for many students they base their intelligence on their performance in school. However, there are many students who have aptitudes or intelligence for activities and tasks beyond the scope of what is tested in school.

Dr Howard Gardner proposes that there are different types of intelligence, and that we tend to use one or two of them to learn. These "intelligences", he claims, are common to us all irrespective of differences in our culture, education or ability as a learner. While our school systems tend to focus on teaching and assessing verbal-linguistic and logical-mathematical intelligences, there are other intelligences that exist.

- **Verbal-linguistic:** an ability with words and languages. Someone with a good verbal memory typically good at reading, writing, storytelling and learning languages. These learners tend to learn best by speaking, listening to others and discussing, reading and writing.
- **Logical-mathematical:** an ability to use logic and reasoning, and recognize abstract patterns, think scientifically and perform complex numerical calculations. These learners tend to learn by problem-solving, using formulas and symbols, and through categorizing and sequencing activities.
- **Musical:** a sensitivity to sounds, rhythms and music, and an ability to sing, compose and play musical instruments. These learners often have strong auditory skills and learn by listening or using rhymes, chants and songs.
- **Visual-spatial:** an ability to think in images and pictures. These learners tend to learn through activities involving pictures and images, colours and patterns, MindMaps and other visual forms.
- **Bodily-kinesthetic:** an ability to use and control bodily movements precisely and handle objects skillfully. These learners often learn best by physical activities such as drama, role plays, sports, dance, gestures and exercises.

- **Interpersonal:** an ability to understand, communicate and empathize with other people and work well as part of a group. These learners tend to be extrovert and outgoing and learn best by working with others in collaborative and cooperative activities such as discussions and group projects.
- **Intrapersonal:** an ability to understand oneself and interpret one's own emotions, feelings, motivations, strengths and weaknesses and what makes you unique. These learners tend to be reserved, intuitive, self-motivated and learn though quiet reflection and thinking and activities involving concentration and higher-order reasoning.
- **Naturalist:** an ability to relate information to one's natural surroundings. These learners tend to learn through activities relating to the outdoors or natural world such as observing wildlife, and monitoring changes and defining distinctions between things.

ACTIVITY

ATL skills: communication, reflection, thinking, transfer

 Time: 30 minutes to 1 hour

 Individual

CONSIDERING YOUR DIFFERENT INTELLIGENCES

Looking at the list above, make your own list of where you feel your intelligences or aptitudes lie.

Now looking at your own list above, think about how you can use these strengths to help you succeed in your learning within the school context. For example, you may think that if you are logical-mathematically minded, then writing essays may be challenging for you. But you have seen in Chapter 2, "Essay writing skills", that many texts you are asked to write have clear patterns to their structures and even to their language, so if you use your mathematical and logical brain to help you focus on these patterns you can succeed in producing good essays.

Intelligence/aptitude	How I can apply it to my learning?

Your learning style

Use the table below to focus on your preferred **sensory style**.

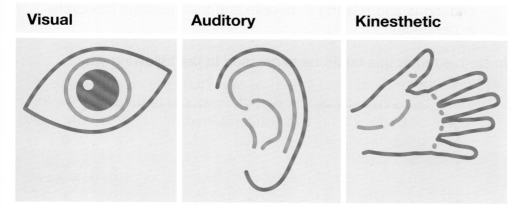

Visual	Auditory	Kinesthetic

Other ways of thinking about and approaching your learning

Throughout the earlier chapters you have been considering your learning style and how you work. Let us now consider two theories on learning styles from well-known experts in this field, and think about how you might fit into their models of learning.

Anthony Gregorc theorized that there are four basic learning styles.

1. **Concrete sequential (CS)** learners who are factual and work hard, approaching tasks in an organized and consistent manner.
2. **Abstract sequential (AS)** learners who are knowledgeable, analytical, thorough and approach tasks in a logical, structured and systematic manner.
3. **Abstract random (AR)** learners who are sensitive, perceptive and imaginative, and who are flexible and spontaneous in the way they approach tasks.
4. **Concrete random (CR)** learners who are creative, intuitive, curious, and who approach tasks in an innovative, adventurous and instinctive manner.

Which of these four best describes you as a learner? Can you think of examples of how you learn in this way?

Fairly similar to this model is David Kolb's model of experiential learning (learning resulting from experiences), in which he classifies learners in terms of:

- how they **process information** or approach a task—learning by doing (active experimentation) or learning by watching, reflecting and seeking meaning in things (reflective observation)

- how they **respond to information** or tasks—by thinking and analysing an idea before acting on their understanding of it (abstract conceptualization) or learning by experiencing real situations and relating to people and their feelings (concrete experience).

In simple terms this could be expressed in the following way.

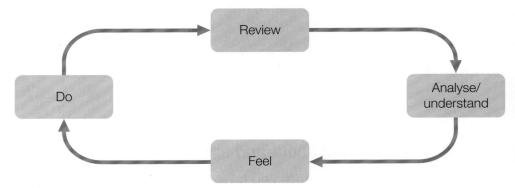

This model has also been adapted to include another stage PLAN so you are thinking about the next stage in the process.

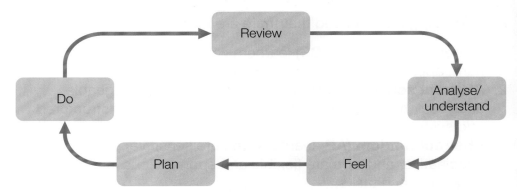

Depending on the task or activity and your ability, motivation and attitude towards it, you may approach it from any starting point on the cycle. For example, when learning a new language you may be someone who has the confidence to jump in and start trying to speak it straight away (**do**) before reflecting on how well you were understood (**review**), reading textbooks to understand how you could communicate better (**analyse/understand**), getting tips from an expert in the language (**feel**) and then planning how you will start practising speaking the language (**plan**). Alternatively, if feeling less confident, you may begin by reading the textbook and studying the language (analyse/understand) and move on from there. No matter the order in which you approach tasks, the key is to follow these steps as you do so.

Collaborative learning

Think back to your childhood when you learned something with the help of a family member or a friend. It could be an activity such as learning to ride a bicycle, learning to get dressed, learning to brush your teeth, tie your shoelaces, hold a pen, play a musical instrument, throw or kick a ball, learning your multiplication tables or something similar.

Using the following questions, think carefully about what helped you succeed in your learning.

- What helped you succeed and learn what to do?
- How did the attitude and response of the person who was helping you affect your progress?
- How motivated did you feel to learn?
- In what emotional state did you learn best?
- How did you feel once you had mastered the skill you were learning?
- What sorts of advice were most helpful?
- What, if any, factors hindered your progress?

Often, as children, we experience ideal circumstances for collaborative learning:

- a supportive nurturing environment
- plenty of positive reinforcement
- modelling of how to do something
- a chance to practise with the help and encouragement of someone more experienced
- a chance to ask questions without feeling stupid
- opportunities to talk about, do and immediately reflect on what has been learned.

Being relaxed, curious, motivated, challenged and supported are the ideal conditions for collaborative work. Think about how you could use opportunities for collaborative learning in your own work.

PULLING IT ALL TOGETHER

These are just some of the many factors that distinguish us all as individuals and make us unique as learners in both the way we prefer to learn and the way we see the world. All of these factors will affect the way you approach a task. In considering the factors above you may have realized that there are many different aspects of your personality, habits, learning styles and approaches to learning that contribute to the way you learn and the way you see and interpret the world.

So how can we make sense of these learning styles and strategies? An important skill in the learning process is being able to organize, synthesize and summarize information. So let us now try and see if we can do that. Below is one approach—a diagram that attempts to illustrate the many influences on us that shape our beliefs, values and attitudes to learning, as well as the approaches and learning strategies we adopt.

Influences on you as a learner

Thinking back on what you have read and seen so far, add to the list below those things that influence you as a learner.

The type of learner I am and my learning skills and strategies
My intelligences (musical, visual-spatial, etc),
my sensory learning preferences (visual, auditory, kinesthetic),
memory techniques, note-making/review techniques, my skills
in exams

Background/ experiences

Cultural upbringing

Family background

Religion

Schooling

Setbacks

Challenges

Exposure to positive role models

Peers

HOW I KNOW
Expectations, values, beliefs, attitudes

HOW I LEARN
Metacognitive skills
Cognitive skills
Affective skills

Study habits
Working alone/ in a group
Study environment
Location
Time of day
Temperature
Distractions
Noise

Personality/lifestyle
The ways I manage my mood, motivation, anxieties, distractions
My other commitments, my self-belief, my response to setbacks,
my willingness to take risks, my character (introvert/extrovert)

If you are a visual learner you may have found this activity suited you. However, if your learning preference was auditory or kinesthetic it may have been harder for you. The key to developing as a learner is to develop your range of strategies for processing information and tackling different tasks. One way of doing this is to think of other ways in which you could organize this information—for example, you might select any of the following.

- A mindmap
- A chart or table
- A mnemonic
- A song, chant or rhyme

Select an approach that may not be one of your strongest strategies and re-present the information above in that form. You may come up with different headings and categories to organize the information.

Having thought about your learning style and the way in which you interpret the world, let us examine your overall abilities as a learner using a tool you should be familiar with from your MYP course— the IB learner profile.

LEARNER PROFILE EXERCISE

The IB learner profile is one way of assessing your skills as a learner. It describes itself "as a set of qualities that could also enhance learning". Using the learner profile published in the front of the book, rank yourself against the 10 learner profile characteristics, placing those you consider as your strengths at the top (on page 214) and those you consider less reflective of you at the bottom.

Begin by deciding on your two strongest and two weakest and then work on placing the others in the middle rows.

ACTIVITY

ATL skills: reflection, thinking

Time: 20 minutes

Individual or class

Characteristics: Inquirer, knowledgeable, critical thinker, communicator, principled, open-minded, caring, risk-taker balanced, reflective.

_____ _____

_____ _____ _____

_____ _____ _____

_____ _____

Now choose one of the qualities at the top of your list and get together with other members of your class who shared that trait. Discuss the following questions.

- What factors made you decide on this as your most characteristic quality?
- What are some of the behaviours that reflect this quality in your life and work?
- What was your other top quality? Can you see any connections?
- What were your least reflective traits? Can you see any connections between them both or between them and your strongest ones?

Focusing on one of the qualities you put at the bottom of your list, read the description in the front of the book about your quality and think about different strategies, attitudes and behaviours that could help you develop this quality in your learning.

CONSIDERING COMMENTS ON LEARNING

Read the statements about learning below and choose three to discuss with a partner. Then, explain:

a) what the statement is saying
b) what important aspects of learning it highlights
c) whether you (dis)agree with it or why you (dis)like it
d) how it relates to your own experience.

Be prepared to share your thoughts with the class, if called on by your teacher.

- *"Learning is not attained by chance, it must be sought for with ardour and attended to with diligence."* Abigail Adams
- *"The purpose of learning is growth, and our minds, unlike our bodies, can continue growing as long as we live."* Mortimer Adler
- *"Learning how to learn is life's most important skill."* Anon
- *"I am learning all the time. The tombstone will be my diploma."* Eartha Kitt
- *"One of the reasons people stop learning is that they become less and less willing to risk failure."* John W Gardner
- *"Develop a passion for learning. If you do, you will never cease to grow."* Anthony J D'Angelo
- *"Anyone who stops learning is old, whether at 20 or 80. Anyone who keeps learning stays young. The greatest thing in life is to keep your mind young."* Henry Ford
- *"We learn more by looking for the answer to a question and not finding it than we do from learning the answer itself."* Lloyd Alexander

- *"Curiosity is the wick in the candle of learning."* William A Ward
- *Every act of conscious learning requires the willingness to suffer an injury to one's self-esteem. That is why young children, before they are aware of their own self-importance, learn so easily."* Thomas Szasz
- *"Only the curious will learn and only the resolute overcome the obstacles to learning. The quest quotient has always excited me more than the intelligence quotient."* Doris Lessing
- *"I never teach my pupils; I only attempt to provide the conditions in which they can learn."* Albert Einstein
- *"Your best teacher is your last mistake."* Ralph Nader
- *"In its broadest sense, learning can be defined as a process of progressive change from ignorance to knowledge, from inability to competence, and from indifference to understanding."* Cameron Fincher

YOUR LEARNING JOURNEY

Hopefully what you have learned by reading this book is that your **A**pproach **to L**earning is dependent on a number of factors, also expressed as "ATLs".

- Your **a**ttitude **to l**ife
- Your **a**bility **to l**earn from your own experiences (successes and failures)
- Your **a**wareness of and **a**ttitude **to**wards your **l**imitations
- Your **a**daptability **to** new life experiences and situations (groups, classes, cultures, knowledge)
- Your **a**bility **to l**ook critically at what you have done and see how it can help you improve

Can you think of other **A T L**s that impact on your learning? Add them to the list.

By now you should have a clearer understanding of what type of a learner you are, your preferred learning styles, approaches and environment, and have some ideas of strategies you can use to improve your learning. By using this book you are starting to think more about your learning style and the ways in which you process and respond to information and to tasks you are given.

Remember the key steps to becoming a better learner.

- Be motivated, flexible, creative and critical about how you learn.
- Try to adopt the qualities of successful learners by being relaxed, focused, motivated and adaptable, willing to develop and try out different approaches to different tasks and stages of learning.
- Then reflect on your learning—what went well and what strategies and approaches didn't work—monitor your progress, and develop your skills in selecting the right strategies to suit the different tasks you are given.
- Actively work on improving your cognitive, metacognitive and affective skills.

On your learning journey, you will suffer setbacks and failures, but how you respond to these is the key. Learning from your mistakes and accepting that developing your skills as a learner is an ongoing process will help you progress and move forward through school and university—and even beyond.

We hope this book has helped you take a small step on that journey.

Useful websites

Hemispheric dominance inventory (L/R)

http://www.mtsu.edu/~studskl/hd/learn.html
http://brain.web-us.com/brain/braindominance.htm

Sensory learning style (auditory, visual, tactile/kinesthetic)

http://www.ulc.arizona.edu/learn_styl_ass.html
http://www.metamath.com/lsweb/dvclearn.htm

Multiple intelligences (eight intelligences)

http://www.ldrc.ca/projects/miinventory/miinventory.php

Sternberg-Wagner (thinking styles inventory)

www.ldrc.ca/projects/tscale/index.php

Index of learning styles (ILS)

www2.ncsu.edu/unity/lockers/users/f/felder/public/ILSdir/ilsweb.html

Excellent online interactive learning style exercise from James Cook University Australia (also based on ILS)

http://www.thelearningweb.net/personalthink.html

Discovery wheel online (Houghton-Mifflin College Site)

http://college.hmco.com/masterstudent/series/master_student_canadian/4e/students/index.html

References

Biggs, J. 1999. *Teaching for Quality Learning at University*. Buckingham, UK. Open University Press.

Blackwell, L., Trzesniewski, K. and Dweck, C.S. 2007. "Implicit theories of intelligence predict achievement across an adolescent transition: A longitudinal study and an intervention". *Child Development*. Vol 78. Pp. 246–263, study 2.

Claxton, G. 1999. *Wise up: the challenge of lifelong learning*. London, UK. Bloomsbury.

Dewey, J. (1933), *How we Think*, Chicago, USA. Henry Regney.

Dweck, C. et al. 2006. "Why do beliefs about intelligence influence learning success? A social cognitive neuroscience model". *Social Cognitive and Affective Neuroscience*. Vol 1, Issue 2. Pp. 75–86.

Guild, P. 1998. *"Diversity, Learning Style and Culture"*. 2nd edition. Adapted from *Marching To Different Drummers* by Pat Burke Guild and Stephen Garger. Alexandria, Virginia, USA. ASCD.

Hinett, K. 2002. Improving Learning through Reflection, Part 1 York: Higher Education Academy [http:www.new1.heacademy.ac.uk/assets/Documents/resources/database/id485_imprving_learning_part_one.pdf]

Kolb, D. 1984. *Experiential Learning: Experience as a Source of Learning and Development*. London, UK. Kogan Page.

Race, P. 2002. *Evidencing Reflection: putting the w into reflection* http://escalate.ac.uk/resources/reflection/

Connor, M. *Introduction to Learning Styles* http://marciaconner.com/resources/learning-styles-intro/ This is an excellent site for assessment tests in engagement styles.

Interview with Dr. Carol Dweck—Developing a Growth Mindset http://www.highlightsparents.com/parenting_perspectives/interview_with_dr_carol_dweck_developing_a_growth_mindset

Krakovsky, M. *The Effort Effect* http://www.stanfordalumni.org/news/magazine/2007/marapr/features/dweck.html

http://www.stanford.edu/dept/psychology/cgi-bin/drupalm/system/files/cdwecklearning%20success.pdf

Kolb's Learning Styles and Experiential Learning Model http://www.nwlink.com/~donclark/hrd/styles.html

MYP COMMAND TERMS

Command terms	MYP definitions
Analyse	Break down in order to bring out the essential elements or structure. To identify parts and relationships, and to interpret information to reach conclusions.
Annotate	Add brief notes to a diagram or graph.
Apply	Use knowledge and understanding in response to a given situation or real circumstances.
Appraise	To evaluate, judge or consider text or a piece of work.
Argue	Challenge or debate an issue or idea with the purpose of persuading or committing someone else to a particular stance or action.
Calculate	Obtain a numerical answer showing the relevant stages in the working.
Classify	Arrange or order by class or category.
Comment	Give a judgment based on a given statement or result of a calculation.
Compare	Give an account of the similarities between two (or more) items or situations, referring to both (all) of them throughout.
Compare and contrast	Give an account of the similarities and differences between two (or more) items or situations, referring to both (all) of them throughout.
Construct	Develop information in a diagrammatic or logical form.
Contrast	Give an account of the differences between two (or more) items or situations, referring to both (all) of them throughout.
Deduce	Reach a conclusion from the information given.
Define	Give the precise meaning of a word, phrase, concept or physical quantity.
Demonstrate	Prove or make clear by reasoning or evidence, illustrating with examples or practical application.
Derive	Manipulate a mathematical relationship to give a new equation or relationship.

Command terms	MYP definitions
Describe	Give a detailed account or picture of a situation, event, pattern or process.
Design	Produce a plan, simulation or model.
Determine	Obtain the only possible answer.
Discuss	Offer a considered and balanced review that includes a range of arguments, factors or hypotheses. Opinions or conclusions should be presented clearly and supported by appropriate evidence.
Distinguish	Make clear the differences between two or more concepts or items.
Document	To credit sources of information used by referencing (or citing) following one recognized referencing system. References should be included in the text and also at the end of the piece of work in a reference list or bibliography.
Estimate	Find an approximate value for an unknown quantity.
Evaluate	To assess the implications and limitations; to make judgments about the ideas, works, solutions or methods in relation to selected criteria.
Examine	Consider an argument or concept in a way that uncovers the assumptions and interrelationships of the issue.
Exemplify	Represent with an example.
Explain	Give a detailed account including reasons or causes.
Explore	Undertake a systematic process of discovery.
Formulate	Express precisely and systematically the relevant concept(s) or argument(s).
Identify	Provide an answer from a number of possibilities. Recognize and state briefly a distinguishing fact or feature.
Infer	Deduce; reason from premises to a conclusion. Listen or read beyond what has been literally expressed.
Interpret	Use knowledge and understanding to recognize trends and draw conclusions from given information.

Command terms	MYP definitions
Investigate	Observe, study or make a detailed and systematic examination, in order to establish facts and reach new conclusions.
Justify	Give valid reasons or evidence to support an answer or conclusion.
Label	Add title, labels or brief explanation(s) to a diagram or graph.
List	Give a sequence of brief answers with no explanation.
Measure	Find the value for a quantity.
Outline	Give a brief account.
Predict	Give an expected result of an upcoming action or event.
Present	Offer for display, observation, examination or consideration.
Prove	Use a sequence of logical steps to obtain the required result in a formal way.
Recall	Remember or recognize from prior learning experiences.
Recognize	Identify through patterns or features.
Reflect	To think about deeply; to consider.
Show	Give the steps in a calculation or derivation.
Sketch	Represent by means of a diagram or graph (labelled as appropriate). The sketch should give a general idea of the required shape or relationship, and should include relevant features.
Solve	Obtain the answer(s) using appropriate methods.
State	Give a specific name, value or other brief answer without explanation or calculation.
Suggest	Propose a solution, hypothesis or other possible answer.
Summarize	Abstract a general theme or major point(s).
Synthesize	Combine different ideas in order to create new understanding.
Use	Apply knowledge or rules to put theory into practice.